JAMIE OLIVER
TOGETHER

Photography DAVID LOFTUS, LEVON BISS & PAUL STUART

Design JAMES VERITY

MICHAEL JOSEPH

Dedicated
to the

NHS

& KEYWORKERS

FOR LOOKING AFTER US AND
KEEPING THE NATION GOING,
ENABLING US TO GET BACK

together

'TOGETHER'

feels more poignant in 2021 than ever before.

What we've been through, collectively, is very unusual, and I think a lot of us have realized that perhaps we took some of life's simple pleasures for granted. Being together is precious. To be in a loved one's presence, to see their face light up, share memories and laugh out loud together, that's what life is truly all about.

And the joyful, amazing thing about food is that it can be anything you want it to be. It can nourish, sustain, help to heal, be fast or convenient, comforting, fun, surprising, or an adventure. But maybe, in its simplest form, it works as an excuse to bring the people you love together. This book is dedicated to just that.

Think good old-fashioned dinner parties, celebrations, special occasions, or just getting your nearest and dearest over for that wonderful end-of-the-week meal. My sole intention here is to arm you with the most trusted, well-thought-out recipes, each written in a specific way to allow you to get organized and ahead of the game, be cool, calm, collected and, most importantly, enjoy your guests. No more being stuck in the kitchen, stressed, sweating and pretending that you're having a great time!

I want to empower you to get into the creative flow and rhythm of planning a really memorable meal. It can be a little bit fancy, or humble and super relaxed, whether it's simply you and a loved one, a small gathering, or more of a crowd living it up. I'll show you what dishes go together well, from the most amazing starters, mains, sides and desserts, peppered with nibbles and cocktails, to inspiration for setting the table and serving up – these are some of my favourite feasts, ones that make me truly happy.

So, please do use the recipes in these pages as an excuse to reconnect with those you've missed seeing, in the intimacy of your home. Celebrate the power that food has to bring people together, remember the immense joy it can bring, and, more than anything, bank those memories with your loved ones. This is about saying 'I love you' through food.

MEMORABLE MEALS MADE EASY

Each chapter starts with a little menu card for that meal – please take a photo of it and you can use it as an invitation to get people over or, of course, you can pick and choose recipes to build your own menu. I've written each individual recipe so it works not only as a component in the wider meal, but as a standalone dish, giving you maximum flexibility. To guarantee that your meal is as stress-free as possible, recipe methods are signposted as follows:

GET AHEAD refers to jobs that can be done the day before your meal, and in some instances, even a couple of days before – this is about getting as much of the hands-on, messy stuff out of the way, in advance. Sometimes we're even cooking ahead, ready to simply reheat and enjoy the next day. I have also flagged where something can just as easily be done on the day, in case you're more of a last-minute person, or want to organize your time in a different way.

ON THE DAY refers to jobs that can be done in advance, but are best done the same day that you're enjoying your meal – it might be prep, it might be the early stages of cooking, but it's certainly stuff that doesn't need to be done in the company of guests.

TO SERVE – you guessed it – this is what you need to do to get the food on the table. Some last-minute prep, some cooking, some garnishing and finishing, it varies from meal to meal.

When it comes to timings, if you choose to follow a whole meal, I'd recommend deciding on the time you want to eat, then working backwards and making a plan of what needs to be done, so you feel totally in control. If you can delegate some jobs, too, that's always a bonus.

PANTRY INGREDIENTS

As with all my recent books, I presume you've got these five everyday staples in the cupboard. They pop up regularly throughout the book and aren't included in each individual ingredients list. They are olive oil for cooking, extra virgin olive oil for dressing and finishing dishes, red wine vinegar as a good all-rounder when it comes to acidity and balancing marinades, sauces and dressings, and sea salt and black pepper for seasoning.

CONTENTS

1

BRUNCH
PARTY

To share

HONEY FOCACCIA

JERKED ROAST PORK

& golden gnarly squash

EASY BAKED EGGS

SUBLIME KALE SALAD

PERFECT PEPPER PICKLE

Pud

PILLOWY MERINGUES

With roasted pineapple, yoghurt & pistachio dust

Drink

PEACH TEA JUG

Anything goes at brunch. Be big, be bold and be confident. Gather your

favourite people together. Be hospitable, be generous, and above all, be happy.

HONEY FOCACCIA

SOFT, SPONGY & UNDENIABLY MOREISH

SERVES 12

500g strong bread flour, plus extra for dusting

1 x 7g sachet of dried yeast

50g natural yoghurt

3 tablespoons runny honey

optional: 1 sprig of rosemary

GET AHEAD You can do this on the day, if you prefer. Put the flour and 1 level teaspoon of sea salt into a large bowl and make a well in the middle. In a jug, mix the yeast into 300ml of lukewarm water, stir in the yoghurt and 1 tablespoon of honey, and leave for a few minutes. Now, gradually pour the mixture into the well, stirring and bringing in the flour from the outside to form a dough. Knead on a flour-dusted surface, picking the dough up and slapping it back down, for 10 minutes, or until smooth and springy. Place in a lightly oiled bowl, cover and refrigerate overnight. If making on the day, cover with a clean damp tea towel and prove in a warm place for 1 hour, or until doubled in size.

ON THE DAY Lightly oil a deep baking tray (30cm x 40cm). Tip in the dough, pull and stretch it out to fill the tray, then use your fingers to gently push down and create lots of dips and wells. Drizzle with a little olive oil and sprinkle generously with black pepper and a little sea salt, cover the tray with a clean damp tea towel, then prove in a warm place for 1 hour, or until doubled in size.

TO SERVE Preheat the oven to 220°C. Very carefully – to keep the air in the dough – transfer the tray to the bottom of the oven and bake for 25 minutes, or until golden and cooked through. Drizzle and brush with 2 tablespoons of extra virgin olive oil and the remaining honey – I like to use a sprig of rosemary to do this – and move to a board ready to slice.

JERKED ROAST PORK

GOLDEN GNARLY SQUASH

SERVES 8

1 butternut squash (1.2kg)

800g piece of skinless boneless
    pork loin

1½ Scotch bonnet chillies

3 large oranges

1 tablespoon low-salt
    soy sauce

1 tablespoon white wine
    vinegar

1 tablespoon brown sugar

4 spring onions

4 cloves of garlic

4cm piece of ginger

4 sprigs of thyme

1 teaspoon ground allspice

½ teaspoon ground cinnamon

1 whole nutmeg, for grating

GET AHEAD You can prep this on the day, if you prefer. Scrub the squash, carefully halve it lengthways and deseed, then cut into twelve chunky wedges, place in a large roasting tray and cover. Score the fat side of the pork in a criss-cross fashion at 1cm intervals. For the jerk marinade, wearing gloves, deseed the chilli – it's hot! – then place in a blender with the orange juice, soy, vinegar, sugar and 1 tablespoon of olive oil. Trim and add the spring onions, peel and add the garlic and ginger, and strip in the thyme. Add the spices, and a good grating of nutmeg, blitz until smooth and season to perfection. Reserve 4 tablespoons of jerk, then pour the rest into a reusable sandwich bag, add the pork, squeeze the air out, seal and massage well. Refrigerate everything overnight.

TO SERVE Preheat the oven to 180°C. Uncover the squash, drizzle with 1 tablespoon of oil and roast for 1 hour 20 minutes, adding the 4 tablespoons of marinade halfway. Reserving the excess marinade, brown the pork in a small non-stick ovenproof frying pan on a medium-high heat until golden all over, turning with tongs. Roast for 45 minutes, then remove to a plate to rest for 20 minutes. Spoon the fat off the pork pan (save it in a jar for tasty cooking another day), then pour in the reserved marinade and simmer on the hob until thickened, adding splashes of water, if needed, and scraping up any nice sticky bits. Finely slice the pork, pouring any resting juices back into the sauce, then decant the sauce into a little bowl to serve. Put the squash on a nice platter.

VEGGIE LOVE

The jerk squash is an amazing veggie option, but if you want to go all out, you can also replace the pork with a small quartered cauliflower (600g), rubbed with jerk marinade, then roasted for 50 minutes, or until gnarly.

EASY BAKED EGGS

SPRING ONIONS, AVO & TOMATOES

Tasty and super-simple, this is a really brilliant thing to knock together at any time of day. I love cooked avocado, and nestling eggs into other ingredients like this is a lovely, gentle way to cook them.

SERVES 6

6 spring onions

400g ripe mixed-colour cherry tomatoes

2 ripe avocados

6 large eggs

hot chilli sauce, to serve

Trim the spring onions and chop into 2cm lengths, then place in a large shallow non-stick pan on a medium heat with the tomatoes and 1 tablespoon of olive oil, tossing regularly. Carefully halve, destone and peel the avocados, then thickly slice lengthways, add to the pan and season with sea salt and black pepper. Cook for 5 minutes, then nudge things about to make room so you can crack in the eggs. Reduce the heat to medium-low, cover and don't look at it for exactly 5 minutes, then check – I like the yolks soft, but cook to your liking. Serve the pan at the table with a casual splattering of hot chilli sauce. Yum.

SUBLIME KALE SALAD

PINK GRAPEFRUIT, PARSLEY, FETA, ALMONDS & SEEDS

SERVES 6

500g curly kale

2 pink grapefruits

1 bunch of flat-leaf parsley
(30g)

4 tablespoons natural yoghurt

50g feta cheese

50g flaked almonds

30g mixed seeds, such as
pumpkin, sunflower, linseed

30g Parmesan cheese

GET AHEAD Wash and pick through the kale, tearing into small pieces and removing any tough stalks. Pile the kale into a colander, sprinkle with ½ a teaspoon of sea salt (most of this will drain away), then scrunch and massage really well for a good couple of minutes. Leave for 15 minutes, while you top and tail the grapefruits, then, standing them on one of the flat ends, slice off the skin. Segment the fruit and store in the fridge, squeezing the juice from the middle bits into a blender for the dressing. Tear in the top leafy half of the parsley, add the yoghurt and feta, and blitz until smooth. Squeeze the kale well to remove the excess salty liquor. Finely chop on a board, then mix with the dressing, cover and refrigerate overnight. The kale is now transformed.

TO SERVE Toast the almonds and seeds in a non-stick frying pan until lightly golden, then turn the heat off. Spoon some of the dressed kale on to a nice serving platter, sprinkle with some toasted nuts and seeds and add a little grating of Parmesan, then keep repeating this layering process, ensuring every mouthful will be a joy. Dot around the grapefruit segments and serve.

PERFECT PEPPER PICKLE

MUSTARD SEEDS, THYME, CHILLI & GARLIC

I make versions of this pickle all the time, playing with different veg and accent flavours – take it as a principle. It keeps really well in the fridge for 2 to 3 weeks, and I use the tangy pickling liquor in salad dressings and marinades. Of course, you can always halve the quantities and make smaller jars, if you prefer – they make a great gift.

MAKES 2 X 1-LITRE JARS

500ml white wine vinegar

4 teaspoons caster sugar

4 teaspoons mustard seeds

4 red peppers

4 fresh red chillies

4 cloves of garlic

1 large red onion

4 sprigs of thyme

GET AHEAD Pour the vinegar into a small casserole pot with 500ml of water. Add the sugar, mustard seeds and 4 teaspoons of sea salt. Cover with a lid (so your whole house doesn't smell of vinegar!) and bring up to a simmer while you slice the peppers into ½cm rings, removing the seeds and stalks. Halve the chillies lengthways and deseed. Peel and finely slice the garlic. Peel the onion and finely slice into rounds. Add it all to the pan with the thyme, mix well, and compress with something heavy so everything is covered with the hot liquor. Simmer for 1 minute, then turn the heat off and leave to cool. Decant all the veg into clean, dry jars or tubs of your choice and pour over the liquor. Press down well, making sure everything is submerged – top up with a 50:50 ratio of vinegar to water, if needed. Put the lids on and store in the fridge.

PILLOWY MERINGUES

ROASTED PINEAPPLE, YOGHURT & PISTACHIO DUST

SERVES 6

3 large eggs

160g icing sugar

1 ripe pineapple

25g unsalted butter

2 oranges

2 fresh bay leaves

4 green cardamom pods

50g shelled unsalted pistachios

Greek-style yoghurt, to serve

GET AHEAD Preheat the oven to 100°C. Separate the eggs, putting just the whites into a free-standing mixer with a small pinch of sea salt (save the yolks for an omelette another day). Whisk until they form very stiff peaks, then turn the mixer off and sift in 150g of the sugar. Turn the mixer back on, gradually working up to the highest setting, then leave to mix for 5 minutes. Line a baking sheet with greaseproof paper (I dab a tiny bit of mixture under each corner to help it stay flat). Divide the rest of the mixture into six rustic piles, using the back of your spoon to flick up cute little peaks and wafts. Bake for 1 hour, then turn the oven off, leaving the meringues in there to cool overnight.

ON THE DAY Remove the meringues from the oven, then preheat to 180°C. Top and tail the pineapple, then sit it on one of the flat ends and trim off the skin. Quarter it lengthways and remove the core, then chop into 2cm chunks. Place in a large non-stick ovenproof pan on a high heat with the butter. Use a speed-peeler to strip in the orange peel, then squeeze in the juice. Cook for a couple of minutes, then add the bay leaves and transfer to the oven to roast for 30 minutes, or until soft and starting to caramelize.

Crush the cardamom pods in a pestle and mortar and remove the outer shells. Pound up the seeds with the remaining 10g of sugar until fine, then bash in the pistachios until you have a lovely green dust.

TO SERVE Make beautiful portions of meringue, yoghurt and pineapple, sprinkled with dust, or take it all to the table and let people help themselves.

PEACH TEA JUG

— SERVES 6 —

GET AHEAD Pour <u>2 x 415g tins of peaches in juice</u> into a pan on a medium heat with <u>2 English breakfast teabags</u>. Simmer for 5 minutes, then turn the heat off, remove the teabags and leave to cool. Pick most of the leaves from <u>½ a bunch of mint (15g)</u> into a blender, then pour in the cool peach mixture and blitz until smooth. Sieve, then cover and refrigerate overnight.

TO SERVE Fill a large jug with ice and pour in <u>200ml each of ginger beer and dark spiced rum</u>, followed by the peach tea. Stir gently and garnish with the remaining mint. Taste, tweaking with extra dashes of ginger beer and a nice little squeeze of <u>lime juice</u>, if you like.

2

LAID-BACK

FEAST

Starter

WONDERFUL WARM SALAD

Sweet red onions, roasted grapes & goat's cheese

Main

CHICKEN, SAUSAGE & BACON PUFF PIE

*With English mustard, leek & watercress sauce,
spring veg & veg à la Grecque*

Pud

RHUBARB & CUSTARD FLOATING ISLANDS

One of the gifts of the cook is being able to subtly tweak comfort food with

a lightness of touch, embracing seasonal ingredients with love and care.

WONDERFUL WARM SALAD

SWEET RED ONIONS, ROASTED GRAPES & GOAT'S CHEESE

SERVES 4

2 red onions

1 bulb of garlic

250g seedless grapes

4 fresh bay leaves

1 teaspoon Dijon mustard

1 red chicory

1 green chicory

1 small frisée lettuce

½ a bunch of tarragon (10g)

4 slices of rustic French
baguette (125g)

60g crumbly goat's cheese

GET AHEAD You can do this on the day, if you prefer. Preheat the oven to 180°C. Peel the onions and slice into 1cm-thick rounds. Halve the unpeeled garlic bulb across the middle. Place in a snug-fitting roasting dish with the grapes, bay and a pinch of sea salt and black pepper, drizzle with 1 tablespoon each of olive oil and red wine vinegar, add 100ml of water, then gently toss to coat. Arrange in a fairly even layer and roast for 45 minutes, or until everything is beautifully soft. Leave to cool, cover with tin foil and refrigerate overnight.

TO SERVE Preheat the oven to 180°C. Pop the covered onion tray in for 10 minutes, to warm through. Mix the mustard with 1 tablespoon of red wine vinegar and 2 tablespoons of extra virgin olive oil, then season to perfection. Trim the chicory and finely slice the base ends, clicking the leaves apart, tear up the white inner leaves of the frisée, then toss it all gently in the dressing and divide between your plates. Pick the tarragon leaves. Toast the bread, squeeze over the soft garlic and mash into the surface, then crumble over the goat's cheese. Add to your plates, spoon over the onions and grapes, along with any juices from the tray, and finish with tarragon leaves.

CHICKEN, SAUSAGE & BACON PUFF PIE

ENGLISH MUSTARD, LEEKS & WATERCRESS SAUCE

SERVES 4

2 rashers of smoked streaky bacon

2 chicken thighs (100g each), skin off, bone out

2 sausages

2 leeks

2 small potatoes (100g each)

2 heaped teaspoons English mustard

2 heaped tablespoons plain flour

500ml chicken stock

500ml semi-skimmed milk

85g watercress

320g ready-rolled puff pastry

1 large egg

GET AHEAD You can do this on the day, if you prefer. Slice the bacon and place in a large shallow casserole pan on a medium heat. Chop the chicken and sausages into 3cm chunks, and add to the pan. Cook until lightly golden, stirring regularly, while you trim and wash the leeks, peel the potatoes, chop it all into 3cm chunks, then stir in with a good splash of water. Cook for 10 minutes, or until the leeks have softened, stirring occasionally, scraping up any sticky bits, and adding an extra splash of water, if needed. Stir in the mustard and flour, followed by the stock, then the milk. Bring to the boil, simmer for 15 minutes on a low heat, stirring regularly, then season to perfection, tasting and tweaking. Carefully pour everything through a colander to separate the filling from the sauce. Pour the sauce into a blender, add the watercress and blitz until smooth. Spoon the filling into a 20cm pie dish with 100ml of sauce. Let everything cool, then cover and refrigerate overnight.

TO SERVE Preheat the oven to 180°C. Brush the rim of the pie dish with olive oil. Cut the pastry into 2cm-thick strips, using a crinkly pasta cutter if you've got one, then arrange over the dish – I like a messy lattice. Eggwash all the pastry, then bake the pie for 45 minutes, or until the pastry is golden and the filling is piping hot. Gently heat up the watercress sauce to serve on the side.

VEGGIE LOVE

Peel 500g of root veg of your choice, chop into 2–3cm chunks and cook for 20 minutes with the leeks, potatoes, 3 tablespoons of olive oil and the leaves from ½ a bunch of thyme (10g). Use veg stock with the milk, top up with 125ml of sauce on assembly, then finish in the same way.

SPRING VEG

JERSEY ROYALS, PEAS & ASPARAGUS

— SERVES 4 —

ON THE DAY Scrub and cook <u>500g of baby new potatoes, Jersey Royals if you can get them</u>, in a large pan of boiling salted water for 15 minutes, or until soft. Trim <u>1 bunch of asparagus (350g)</u> and cut each spear into three lengths, adding to the pan for the last 3 minutes, along with <u>350g of frozen peas</u> for just the final minute. Drain well, then tip into a serving bowl. Pick, finely chop and add the leaves from <u>½ a bunch of mint (15g)</u>, squeeze over the juice from <u>1 lemon</u>, add 1 tablespoon of extra virgin olive oil and gently toss together, then season to perfection, tasting and tweaking. Delicious hot, warm, or even cold.

VEG À LA GRECQUE

THYME, FENNEL & MUSTARD SEEDS

— SERVES 4 WITH LEFTOVERS —

ON THE DAY Tear <u>6 fresh bay leaves</u> into a large shallow bowl, strip in the leaves from <u>½ a bunch of thyme (10g)</u>, add <u>1 level teaspoon each of fennel and mustard seeds</u>, a good pinch of sea salt and black pepper, and <u>4 tablespoons each of white wine vinegar</u> and extra virgin olive oil. This is for steeping, you won't use it all – leftover liquor is great for salad dressings.

Wash and halve <u>200g of small mixed-colour carrots</u>, then cook in a large pan of boiling water for 3 minutes. Add <u>200g of trimmed green beans</u> and cook for another 3 minutes, then add <u>200g each of radishes, button mushrooms and baby courgettes</u> and cook for a final 3 minutes. Drain well, then pour into the bowl of dressing and toss together well. Serve warm or cold. Leftover veg will keep happily in the fridge, covered, for a few days.

RHUBARB & CUSTARD FLOATING ISLANDS

MERINGUE, STRAWBERRY JAM & TOASTED ALMONDS

150g strawberry jam

400g rhubarb

1 orange

30g flaked almonds

2 large eggs

100g icing sugar

1 litre semi-skimmed milk

1 teaspoon vanilla bean paste

1 x 400g tin of custard

optional: 37g Maltesers

GET AHEAD You can do this on the day, if you prefer. Preheat the oven to 180°C. Spread the jam across the base of a 25cm x 30cm baking dish, then split the rhubarb lengthways, cut into 4cm lengths and add to the dish. Use a speed-peeler to strip in the orange peel, then squeeze in the juice and gently toss together. Bake for 30 minutes, or until soft, then remove, cool, cover and refrigerate overnight. Sprinkle the almonds across a tray, toast in the oven for 5 minutes, or until golden, then remove and cool. Cover and store overnight.

TO SERVE Separate the eggs, putting just the whites into a free-standing mixer with a small pinch of sea salt (save the yolks for an omelette another day). Whisk until they form very stiff peaks, then, turn the mixer off and sift in the sugar. Turn the mixer back on, gradually work up to the highest setting, then leave to mix for 5 minutes. Pour the milk into a large shallow pan on a medium heat with the vanilla paste. Bring to a very gentle simmer, then use a large spoon to divide the meringue mixture into four, gently dropping each spoonful into the simmering milk. Poach for 6 minutes, or until firm and just cooked through, gently turning over halfway, then turn the heat off (strain the leftover milk and you can use it in hot chocolate or smoothies, if you like). Divide the custard between your plates, spooning over the rhubarb and meringues, then scattering with almonds. I like to sprinkle over some crushed Maltesers, too.

LOVE YOUR LEFTOVERS

The rhubarb will be a joy on porridge, with granola and yoghurt, ice cream, or even a pork chop.

CURRY
NIGHT

--------------------------- *To share* ---------------------------

FRAGRANT SQUASH CURRY

GOLDEN PANEER

SMOKY AUBERGINE DAAL

FLUFFY COCONUT RICE

FENNEL NAAN

CHOPPED SALAD

CARROT RAITA & MANGO CHUTNEY

--------------------------- *Pud* ---------------------------

MINTED MANGO FRO-YO

The union of vivacious colours, mellow flavours and surprising texture.

... reates mouthwatering excitement in this Indian-inspired sharing feast.

FRAGRANT SQUASH CURRY

CHICKPEAS, GINGER, SPICES & COCONUT MILK

SERVES 6 + 2 LEFTOVER PORTIONS

1 butternut squash (1.2kg)

1 onion

2 cloves of garlic

4cm piece of ginger

1 teaspoon coriander seeds

1 teaspoon fenugreek seeds

1 teaspoon medium curry powder

300g ripe cherry tomatoes

2 tinned pineapple rings in juice

1 x 400ml tin of light coconut milk

1 x 400g tin of chickpeas

optional: 2 sprigs of coriander, to serve

GET AHEAD You can make this on the day, if you prefer. Preheat the oven to 180°C. Scrub the squash (there's no need to peel it), carefully halve it lengthways and deseed, then chop into 2cm chunks. Place in a roasting tray, toss with 1 tablespoon of olive oil and a pinch of sea salt and black pepper, then roast for 1 hour, or until soft and caramelized.

Meanwhile, peel and roughly chop the onion, peel the garlic and ginger, and dry fry in a non-stick frying pan on a medium-high heat with the coriander and fenugreek seeds and the curry powder, stirring until lightly charred all over. Add the tomatoes and pineapple rings (reserving the juice), and cook for 10 minutes to soften and char, stirring regularly. Tip it all into a blender, add the coconut milk and blitz until very smooth. Return to the pan, tip in the chickpeas, juice and all, and simmer gently until the sauce is thickened. Stir in the roasted squash, then season the curry to perfection, tasting and tweaking, and loosening with the reserved pineapple juice. Cool, cover and refrigerate overnight.

TO SERVE Preheat the oven to 150°C. Place the covered pan of curry in the oven until hot through – about 1 hour. Nice with picked coriander leaves.

GOLDEN PANEER

SENSATIONAL TANGY SPINACH CURRY

SERVES 6

1 red onion

2 cloves of garlic

4cm piece of ginger

2 fresh green chillies

1 heaped teaspoon garam masala

1 tablespoon mango chutney

200g spinach

4 tablespoons natural yoghurt

200g paneer cheese

1 heaped teaspoon ground turmeric

GET AHEAD You can make this on the day, if you prefer. Peel the onion, garlic and ginger. Finely slice the onion, 1 clove of garlic, half the ginger and 1 chilli. Place in a non-stick frying pan on a medium heat with 1 tablespoon of olive oil. Fry for 5 minutes, stirring regularly, then stir in the garam masala and mango chutney, followed by the spinach. Let it wilt, then tip the contents of the pan into a blender. Add 2 tablespoons of yoghurt, blitz until smooth, then season to perfection, tasting and tweaking. Cool, cover and refrigerate overnight.

Meanwhile, chop the paneer into 2cm chunks and place in a bowl with the turmeric and ½ a tablespoon of oil. Finely grate over the remaining garlic and ginger and toss gently to coat. Cover and marinate in the fridge overnight.

TO SERVE Fry the paneer in a non-stick frying pan, turning with tongs until golden all over. Prick the remaining chilli and blacken alongside, then remove. Pour in the spinach sauce and simmer for 5 minutes, loosening with splashes of water, if needed. Ripple through the remaining 2 tablespoons of yoghurt, then serve with the blackened chilli and an extra sprinkling of turmeric, if you like.

SMOKY AUBERGINE DAAL

LENTILS, BLACK BEANS, SAVOURY SPICE & ROSEMARY

SERVES 6 + 2 LEFTOVER PORTIONS

1 large aubergine (400g)

1 fresh red chilli

2 cloves of garlic

1 red onion

2 black cardamom pods

1 teaspoon cumin seeds

1 teaspoon black mustard
seeds

1 small sprig of rosemary

1 x 400g tin of black beans

200g dried Puy lentils

1 cinnamon stick

GET AHEAD Prick the aubergine, then lightly blacken it directly over a flame on the hob or in a hot griddle pan, turning with tongs. Remove to a board.

Halve the chilli lengthways and deseed, peel and finely slice the garlic, then peel and finely chop the onion. Crush the cardamom pods in a pestle and mortar and remove the outer shells, then pound up the seeds. Place a large non-stick ovenproof frying pan on a medium-low heat with 1 tablespoon of olive oil and the cumin, mustard and cardamom seeds. Strip in the rosemary and let it gently sizzle for a few minutes, infusing the oil and allowing the flavours to mingle. Add the chilli, garlic and onion and cook for 5 minutes, or until softened, stirring regularly. Chop the aubergine into 3cm chunks and stir into the pan, then add 1 tablespoon of red wine vinegar. Let it sizzle for a couple of minutes, then pour in the beans, juice and all, the lentils and 600ml of water. Set fire to the cinnamon stick, then sit it in the centre of the pan. Cover the daal and leave to thicken on a medium-low heat for 1 hour, loosening with splashes of water, if needed, and stirring occasionally. Season to perfection, tasting and tweaking, then cool, cover the pan and refrigerate overnight.

TO SERVE Preheat the oven to 150°C. Place the covered pan of daal into the oven until hot through – about 1 hour. Stir well, and serve.

FLUFFY COCONUT RICE

CARDAMOM, LEMON & SAFFRON-INFUSED MILK

SERVES 6

3 tablespoons desiccated
coconut

450g basmati rice

1 lemon

150ml semi-skimmed milk

1 pinch of saffron

1 small knob of unsalted
butter or ghee

6 green cardamom pods

GET AHEAD You can make this on the day, if you prefer. Toast the coconut in a pan until lightly golden, tossing regularly, then remove. Put the rice into the same pan, cover with boiling kettle water and boil for 6 minutes, then cool quickly under cold running water and drain well. Tip into a bowl, squeeze over the lemon juice, add the toasted coconut and a big pinch of sea salt and black pepper and mix well, then cover and refrigerate overnight.

TO SERVE Gently heat the milk, adding the saffron to infuse. Rub the butter across the base of a cold 26cm non-stick frying pan, then sprinkle in the cardamom pods. Tip in the rice, then use your hands to shape into a dome. Use the handle of a wooden spoon to poke a few holes deep into the dome to help the rice steam and create vessels, so you can spoon in the warm saffron milk. Cover carefully with a scrunched-up sheet of damp greaseproof paper. Use tin foil to tightly seal the pan, then cook over a low heat for 20 minutes, or until the base is crispy and the rice is fluffy and hot through.

FENNEL NAAN

BUTTERY, SOFT FLATBREAD

SERVES 6

500g strong white bread flour

1 x 7g sachet of dried yeast

1 teaspoon runny honey

3 teaspoons fennel seeds

20g unsalted butter or ghee

GET AHEAD You can do this on the day, if you prefer. Put the flour and 1 level teaspoon of sea salt into a large bowl and make a well in the middle. In a jug, mix the yeast into 375ml of lukewarm water with the honey and leave for a few minutes. Now, gradually pour the mixture into the well, stirring and bringing in the flour from the outside to form a dough. Knead on a flour-dusted surface, picking the dough up and slapping it back down, for 10 minutes, or until smooth and springy, then place in a lightly oiled bowl, cover and refrigerate overnight. If making on the day, cover with a clean damp tea towel and prove in a warm place for 1 hour, or until doubled in size.

TO SERVE Lightly crush the fennel seeds in a pestle and mortar. On a flour-dusted surface, split the dough into three equal pieces. Sprinkle the floured surface with 1 teaspoon of fennel seeds, then roll one ball of dough out on top until about 1cm thick. Place in a hot non-stick pan on a high heat, add 1 tablespoon of water to the pan, immediately cover and cook for 3 minutes on each side, or until golden and puffed up – adding the water creates steam and helps it rise. Remove to a board, rub with a little butter and sprinkle with a small pinch of salt, then repeat the process.

CHOPPED SALAD

BOMBAY MIX, CRUNCHY VEG, MINT & ORANGE

— SERVES 6 —

TO SERVE On a large board, trim <u>200g of radishes</u> and <u>2 little gem lettuces</u>, pick over the leaves from <u>2 sprigs of mint</u>, then finely chop it all with <u>½ a cucumber</u>. Squeeze over the juice from <u>1 orange</u> and mix together, then season to perfection, tasting and tweaking. Transfer to a platter, then gently crush <u>2 tablespoons of Bombay mix</u> in a pestle and mortar and scatter over the top.

CARROT RAITA

LEMON & NIGELLA SEEDS

— SERVES 6 —

ON THE DAY Toast <u>2 teaspoons of nigella seeds</u> in a non-stick pan until smelling fantastic. Wash <u>1 large carrot</u>, then coarsely grate into a bowl. Add <u>250g of natural yoghurt</u> and the nigella seeds. Squeeze in the juice from <u>½ a lemon</u> and mix. Season to perfection, tasting and tweaking. Finish with a kiss of extra virgin olive oil, if you like, then cover and refrigerate until needed.

MANGO CHUTNEY

POMEGRANATE JEWELS

— SERVES 6 —

ON THE DAY Halve <u>1 pomegranate</u> and, holding one half cut side down in the palm of your hand, bash the back with a spoon so all the seeds tumble out into a bowl. Squeeze in the juice from the other half through a sieve, stir in <u>4 tablespoons of mango chutney</u>, then finely chop and add a few <u>coriander leaves</u>, if you like.

MINTED MANGO FRO-YO

PISTACHIO DUST & CHOCOLATE

— SERVES 6 —

TO SERVE Make this to order. In a food processor, blitz <u>50g of shelled unsalted pistachios</u> into a fine dust, then tip on to a plate. Crush <u>3 green cardamom pods</u> in a pestle and mortar and remove the outer shells, then pound the seeds until fine and put in the processor with <u>500g of frozen mango chunks</u> and the leaves from <u>1 sprig of mint</u>. Blitz together. With the processor still running, add <u>3 tablespoons of natural yoghurt</u> and the juice of ½ a lime. Now, while it's still frozen and scoopable, gently roll spoonfuls of mixture in the pistachio dust and serve right away. Finish with a grating or shaving of <u>dark chocolate (70%)</u>.

TACO PARTY

4

To share

SLOW-COOKED PORK BELLY

BLACK BEANS & CHEESE

HOMEMADE TORTILLAS

ROASTED PINEAPPLE

HOT RED PEPPER SAUCE

GREEN SALSA

RED CABBAGE

Pud

CHOCOLATE SEMIFREDDO

With hazelnut brittle & spiced dust

Drink

TEQUILA MICHELADA

Some of my favourite food memories are about introducing loved ones to new

...astes from my travels. This Mexican-inspired riot of flavour is always a joy.

SLOW-COOKED PORK BELLY

SERVES 12

Getting ahead is the absolute best thing you can do with this recipe – cooking the pork the day before you need it means all the fats will have solidified so it's easier to slice, and you'll also get a much better flavour. As well as achieving incredible tenderness from the slow cook, you get crispy golden gnarliness from the roast on the day.

4 fresh bay leaves

1 heaped teaspoon each
    smoked paprika, ground
    coriander, ground
    cinnamon, ground allspice

1.5kg piece of boneless pork
    belly, skin off and reserved
    (see tip below)

GET AHEAD Preheat the oven to 180°C. Tear the bay leaves into a pestle and mortar (discarding the stalks), and pound into a mush. Muddle in the spices and 1 teaspoon each of sea salt and black pepper, then loosen with a little olive oil so you can rub it all over the pork belly (leaving the skin as it is for now). Sit the belly in a snug-fitting roasting tray, cover tightly with tin foil and roast for 2 hours. Remove, cool and refrigerate overnight.

ON THE DAY Preheat the oven to 200°C. Season the piece of pork skin with a pinch of salt and pepper, then lay on a baking tray and roast at the top of the oven for 1 hour, or until golden and crunchy. Transfer the pork belly to a board, slice 1cm thick, then lay across a large baking tray (reserving the tray of juices for my Black beans & cheese, page 72). Roast the pork for 30 minutes, or until crisp, sizzling and golden. Carefully drain off any fat from the crackling tray and save in a jar for tasty cooking another day, then snap up the crackling. Serve up at the table with all the sides, ready for taco building.

ASK YOUR BUTCHER

To remove the pork skin in one piece, ready to roast.

VEGGIE LOVE

Scrub 1 butternut squash (1.2kg), carefully halve it lengthways and deseed, then slice 1cm thick and toss with the spice mixture. Roast in a tray on the bottom of the oven at 200°C for 30 minutes, or until soft and golden.

BLACK BEANS & CHEESE

GOLDEN TEQUILA & SPRING ONIONS

— SERVES 12 —

ON THE DAY Preheat the oven to 200°C. I make these beans using the tray of sticky pork juices (page 68) for extra flavour and less washing-up. Remove a spoonful of fat from the tray, then place over a medium-high heat on the hob. Add <u>50ml of golden tequila (optional)</u> or water and use a wooden spoon to scrape up all the sticky goodness. Let the alcohol cook away while you trim and slice <u>2 spring onions</u>. Add them to the tray, then chop and add <u>½ a bunch of coriander (15g)</u>, stalks and all. Pour in <u>2 x 400g tins of black beans</u>, juice and all, and as soon as they start to bubble, season to perfection, tasting and tweaking. Crumble over <u>80g of feta cheese</u>, transfer to the oven, and bake for 30 minutes, or until thick and delicious.

> ### VEGGIE LOVE
> If you want to go veggie, simply start with a clean tray and 1 tablespoon of olive oil.

HOMEMADE TORTILLAS

WHITE MASA HARINA FLOUR

— SERVES 12 —

ON THE DAY You can't beat the smell and taste of homemade tortillas. Measure out 700ml of boiling kettle water and let it cool for 5 minutes. Put <u>500g of white masa harina flour</u> into a large bowl with a pinch of sea salt and make a well in the middle, then pour in the hot water. Use a fork to gradually mix in the flour, until it starts to come together. Bring into a smooth dough, then, once cool enough to handle, divide into six equal pieces and split each sixth into six balls, giving you 36 in total – cover with a clean damp tea towel as you go to prevent them drying out. Tear off a large sheet of greaseproof paper, fold it in half, place one ball in the middle, press down to flatten, and roll it out between the paper until about 2mm thick, then repeat the process, stacking them in sheets of greaseproof paper as you go so they don't dry out. Cook three tortillas at a time for 1 minute on each side in a large dry hot non-stick pan on a medium heat. As they're cooked, stack them up in a clean tea towel so they stay warm until you're ready to tuck in.

ROASTED PINEAPPLE

HOT RED PEPPER SAUCE

— SERVES 12 —

GET AHEAD Preheat the oven to 180°C. Halve and deseed <u>4 fresh red chillies</u>. Peel <u>4 red onions</u>, deseed <u>4 red peppers</u> and cut them all into quarters. Peel and break apart <u>1 bulb of garlic</u>. Put it all into a large high-sided tray or ovenproof pan. Top and tail <u>1 very ripe pineapple</u>, then sit it on one of the flat ends and trim off the skin. Use a small sharp knife to remove the spikes, following the natural diagonal pattern around the fruit, like in the picture above. Halve it lengthways, sit it cut side down in the tray, drizzle with 1 tablespoon of olive oil, add a pinch of sea salt and black pepper and toss to coat. Roast for 1 hour, or until soft and golden, then remove the pineapple. Pour the contents of the tray into a blender, add a splash of red wine vinegar and blitz until smooth, then season to perfection, tasting and tweaking. Decant into a serving bowl. Return the pineapple to the tray. Cool both, cover, and refrigerate overnight.

ON THE DAY Preheat the oven to 200°C. Reheat the pineapple for 30 minutes, ready to carve off chunks (avoiding the core).

GREEN SALSA

TOMATOES, CHILLI & LIME

RED CABBAGE

HERBS & CITRUS

— SERVES 12 —

— SERVES 12 —

ON THE DAY Quarter and deseed <u>1 green pepper</u> and <u>2 large green tomatoes</u>, then finely chop with <u>1 fresh green chilli</u>, <u>2 trimmed spring onions</u> and <u>½ a bunch of coriander (15g)</u>. Keep chopping until fine, mixing as you go. Scrape into a nice bowl, add 2 tablespoons of extra virgin olive oil, squeeze over the juice of <u>1–2 limes</u>, then season to perfection, tasting and tweaking. Cover and refrigerate until needed.

ON THE DAY Take your time to very finely slice <u>¼ of a red cabbage (250g)</u>. Place in a bowl, finely chop and add the leaves from <u>½ a bunch of coriander or mint (15g)</u>, squeeze in the juice of <u>1 lime</u> and <u>1 orange</u>, and add 1 tablespoon of extra virgin olive oil. Toss and scrunch together well, then season to perfection, tasting and tweaking. Cover and refrigerate until needed.

CHOCOLATE SEMIFREDDO

HAZELNUT BRITTLE & SPICED DUST

SERVES 12

100g dark chocolate (70%),
   plus extra to serve

4 large eggs

200ml double cream

100g golden caster sugar

1 x 400g tin of rice pudding

2 tablespoons cocoa powder

GET AHEAD Line a 1.5-litre freezer-proof terrine mould or loaf tin with a double layer of clingfilm, letting it overhang at the edges. Melt the chocolate in a large heatproof bowl over a pan of gently simmering water, making sure the water doesn't touch the base of the bowl. Remove and allow to cool while you separate the eggs. Whisk the egg whites with a pinch of sea salt until super-stiff, then, in a separate bowl, whisk the cream with the sugar until it forms soft peaks. Stir the rice pudding and cocoa into the melted chocolate, then whisk up the egg yolks and fold in with a spatula, followed by the cream. Finally, fold in the whites, working from the outside in and from bottom to top, until fully mixed but being mindful to retain as much air as possible. Pour into the lined mould, fold in the overhanging clingfilm to cover, then freeze overnight.

TO SERVE Move the semifreddo from freezer to fridge 2 hours before you want to eat so you have a semi-frozen, sliceable dessert. Turn it out on to a serving platter, and sprinkle over the Hazelnut brittle (page 78) and Spiced dust (page 78). Nice with shaved or grated chocolate, too.

HAZELNUT BRITTLE

GOLDEN CARAMEL

— SERVES 12 —

GET AHEAD Put <u>200g of golden caster sugar</u> into a pan with 50ml of water and place on a medium-high heat for about 6 minutes, or until you've got a chestnut brown caramel – please don't be tempted to stir, taste or touch the mixture, just give the pan a gentle swirl occasionally. Gently stir in <u>100g of blanched hazelnuts</u>, then pour the mixture on to an oiled baking sheet. Leave to cool, then use a pestle or the end of a rolling pin to smash up the brittle until you've got a mixture of fine and chunky. Cover and store until needed.

SPICED DUST

WONDERFULLY WARMING

— SERVES 12 —

GET AHEAD Put <u>1 level teaspoon each of ground cinnamon, coriander seeds and ground allspice</u> into a pestle and mortar. Crumble in <u>1 dried red chilli</u>, add <u>4 heaped teaspoons of cocoa powder</u> and <u>2 heaped teaspoons of icing sugar</u>, and pound until fine. Sieve the mixture into an airtight jar ready to use. Leftovers will be an absolute treat sprinkled over ice cream or used to make a lovely mug of hot chocolate.

TEQUILA MICHELADA

— SERVES 1 —

TO SERVE Rub the rim of a tall glass with a wedge of <u>lime</u>, then dip it into fine sea salt (Maldon smoked salt would be awesome here). Halve <u>1 large ripe tomato</u> and grate the cut side on a box grater into a perfumed slurry, discarding the skin and seeds. Pour into the glass, along with <u>30ml of golden tequila</u>. Squeeze in the juice from your lime wedge, add a dash of <u>hot chilli sauce</u>, and stir. Drop in a few chunky ice cubes, then top up the glass with <u>cold lager</u>.

5

SUNNY
GATHERING

Nibble

CHEESE PUFFS

Starter

TENDER ASPARAGUS

With glorious green dressing, soft-boiled eggs & crispy bacon croutons

Main

STUFFED SALMON

Served with potato salad, roasted tomatoes & tasty greens

Pud

WIMBLEDON SUMMER PUDDING

Tennis in full swing, the smell of cut grass, luminous flavours, simplicity

and surprise — these are the things that make me smile come summertime.

CHEESE PUFFS

I'm gonna say the C word, canapé. I had my first one at the age of 13 when I was doing work experience in this beautiful restaurant called The Starr in Dunmow. The food was excellent and they would always start the customer's experience with a drink and something to nibble. It was totally logical and exciting – pairing a glass of something delicious with something salty and textured is, for me, the perfect combo. This is my expression of the first canapé I tried, all those years ago.

SERVES 8

50g Parmesan cheese

100g Lincolnshire Poacher or Cheddar cheese

50g unsalted butter

100g plain flour

50g fine semolina

3 large eggs

GET AHEAD Finely grate all of the cheese. Place the butter in a medium pan on a medium heat with 250ml of cold water. As soon as the mixture comes to a rolling boil, tip in the flour, semolina and a pinch of sea salt. With a wooden spoon, work carefully, quickly and fairly vigorously to beat it all together until smooth and starting to come away from the sides of the pan. Remove from the heat and beat for 30 seconds, then, one at a time, beat in the eggs, followed by the grated cheese. Cover and refrigerate for at least 2 hours. Line a baking sheet with greaseproof paper. With wet hands, divide the mixture into 24 pieces and roll into glorious, shiny balls, lining them up on the tray as you go. Cover and return to the fridge overnight.

TO SERVE Preheat the oven to 200°C. Bake uncovered for 20 minutes, or until golden. Enjoy warm with a glass of something cold and sparkling.

THE FREEZER IS YOUR FRIEND

These are fantastic cooked from frozen if you want to get super ahead. Simply bake for 35 minutes at 200°C.

TENDER ASPARAGUS

With glorious green dressing, soft-boiled eggs & crispy bacon croutons

SERVES 8

2 spring onions

2 tablespoons Dijon mustard

2 tablespoons white wine vinegar

1 bunch of flat-leaf parsley (30g)

4 rashers of smoked streaky bacon

200g sourdough bread

1kg asparagus

8 large eggs

GET AHEAD Roughly chop the green part of the spring onions and place in a blender with the mustard, vinegar and 6 tablespoons of extra virgin olive oil. Tear in three-quarters of the parsley leaves, add a swig of water and blitz until smooth. Season to perfection, tasting and tweaking, then cover. Pick the remaining parsley leaves into a bowl, then trim, finely slice and add the whites of the spring onions, and cover with water. Refrigerate both overnight.

ON THE DAY Put a large non-stick frying pan on a medium heat. Finely slice the bacon, chop the bread into 1cm chunks, and place it all in the pan with 1 tablespoon of olive oil and a good pinch of black pepper. Cook for 15 minutes, or until golden and crisp, tossing regularly. Keep in the pan, ready to reheat. Divide the dressing between a large serving bowl and a smaller bowl, ready for drizzling. Snap the woody ends off the asparagus, then cook in a large pan of boiling water for 3 minutes, or until just tender. Use tongs to transfer the asparagus straight into the larger bowl of dressing, tossing to coat. Gently lower the eggs into the boiling water with a pinch of sea salt to cook for 6 minutes, then drain, cool under cold running water, and peel.

TO SERVE Heat up the croutons. Halve the eggs and dot among the asparagus. Drain the parsley and spring onion garnish, pat dry, then scatter over the top, and take everything to the table – the asparagus will be delicious hot, warm or cold. I enjoy this starter with a glass of quality cold sparkling cider.

VEGGIE LOVE

When frying the croutons, swap the bacon for a pinch of smoked paprika.

STUFFED SALMON

What I like about this recipe is that the method, which is incredibly easy to follow, elevates the salmon to a new level. It makes a real event of this incredible fish and, while it cooks, the flavours all mix and mingle together, amplifying utter deliciousness.

SERVES 8

1 heaped tablespoon baby capers in brine

10 anchovy fillets in oil

2 sprigs of rosemary

10 mixed-colour olives

1 fresh red chilli

1 lemon

1.2kg side of salmon, skin on, pin-boned

GET AHEAD You can prep this on the day, if you prefer. Put the capers into a small bowl, then tear in the anchovies and strip in the rosemary leaves. Squash and destone the olives, tearing the flesh into the bowl, then finely slice and add the chilli. Finely grate over the lemon zest, squeeze in the juice, add 2 tablespoons of olive oil, and mix well. Cover and refrigerate overnight.

ON THE DAY Place the salmon skin side down in the middle of your largest roasting tray and use the tip of a small sharp knife to make deep cuts into the flesh at 3cm intervals. Now stuff each cut, using the knife to help you. I start by dividing up the olives and anchovies, then add the rosemary, chilli and capers. Take your time and enjoy the process. Sprinkle any excess around the salmon.

TO SERVE Preheat the oven to 180°C. Roast the salmon at the bottom of the oven for 20 minutes. Let it rest for 10 minutes, then serve.

VEGGIE LOVE

A giant stuffed Portobello mushroom for each veggie guest instead of salmon is a thing of joy – just lose the anchovies.

POTATO SALAD

ENGLISH MUSTARD & LEMON

— SERVES 8 —

ON THE DAY Wash <u>1.6kg of new potatoes</u>, halving any larger ones, then cook in a large pan of boiling salted water for 15 minutes, or until soft. Drain well. Spoon <u>4 heaped tablespoons of natural yoghurt</u> and <u>4 teaspoons of English mustard</u> into a large serving bowl with 2 tablespoons of extra virgin olive oil. Finely grate in the zest of <u>1 lemon</u>, squeeze in the juice, mix well, then toss in the warm potatoes. Season to perfection, tasting and tweaking.

TO SERVE It's fun to sprinkle this dish with edible flower petals, such as marigolds, violas or nasturtiums. Fresh herb flowers would also work a treat. Serve the potatoes hot, warm or cold.

ROASTED TOMATOES

GARLIC & OREGANO

— SERVES 8 —

GET AHEAD Halve <u>1.2kg of ripe mixed-colour cherry tomatoes</u>, placing them in a large roasting tray as you go. Halve <u>1 bulb of garlic</u> across the middle and add to the tray. Pick in the leaves from <u>2 sprigs of oregano</u>, if you've got some, then add 1 tablespoon each of olive oil and red wine vinegar and a pinch of sea salt and black pepper. Toss together and arrange in a single layer. Cover and refrigerate overnight.

TO SERVE Preheat the oven to 180°C. Roast the tomatoes for 1 hour, before you cook the salmon (page 90). Great hot or warm.

TASTY GREENS

BLACKBERRY & FENNEL DRESSING

— SERVES 8 —

GET AHEAD Prep <u>800g of mixed seasonal greens, such as kale, cabbage or chard</u>, discarding any tough stalks. In a small jug, fork up **4 blackberries** into a mush, then mix with 2 tablespoons of red wine vinegar and 4 tablespoons of extra virgin olive oil. Toast <u>½ **a tablespoon of fennel seeds**</u> in a dry frying pan on a medium heat until smelling fantastic, then add to the dressing. Season to perfection, tasting and tweaking, then cover and refrigerate both overnight.

ON THE DAY Blanch each type of greens in a large pan of boiling water until just tender but still full of life, then drain well and leave until cool enough to handle. Pile the greens in the centre of a clean tea towel, wrap them up, and wring out really well to remove the excess liquid.

TO SERVE Unwrap and roughly chop the greens, then toss with the dressing until beautifully coated, and serve at room temperature.

WIMBLEDON SUMMER PUDDING

STRAWBERRIES, PIMM'S, CUCUMBER, GINGER BEER & MINT

SERVES 12

I grew up making and loving summer pudding, and I still adore it now. If I had a tiny criticism, it would be that blackberries, blackcurrants and raspberries can feel a bit seedy, so I love this recipe, which is dedicated to the wonderful combo of strawberries and cream, and nods to the delightful summer drink of Pimm's. The use of cucumber is a game changer – please embrace it, you won't regret it.

400g golden caster sugar

150ml Pimm's

150ml ginger beer

1 vanilla pod

1 cucumber

1kg ripe strawberries

½ a bunch of mint (15g)

11 x 1cm-thick slices of white
bread

clotted cream, to serve

GET AHEAD Put 200g of the sugar into a large non-stick frying pan on a medium heat. As soon as it's melted into a chestnut brown caramel, carefully pour in the Pimm's and ginger beer – the mixture may seize up but don't worry, simmer and stir gently until it comes together. Halve the vanilla pod lengthways and scrape out the seeds, adding both to the pan, let the mixture bubble away for 5 minutes, then turn the heat off. Use a speed-peeler to peel the cucumber, halve it lengthways and scrape out the seeds with a teaspoon, then slice it ½cm thick and, in a bowl, toss with 100g of sugar. Hull, halve and add the strawberries, tossing again. Pick and finely chop half the mint leaves, then gently stir into the caramel with the cucumber and strawberries.

Double line a 2-litre pudding bowl with clingfilm, leaving a generous overhang. Cut the crusts off the bread and cut the pieces in half. Gently dip one side of each piece into the pan of fruit so it sucks up some jammy juice, then place enough slices, jam against clingfilm, to line the sides, then the bottom of the bowl, slightly overlapping them as you go. Use a slotted spoon to pile in the cucumber and strawberries, leaving the juices behind, then double dip the remaining pieces of bread and use them to cover the filling. Fold in the overhanging clingfilm, creating a bit of tension to wrap it tight. Pop a plate on top, as well as something heavy to weigh it down, and refrigerate on a tray for at least 8 hours, or up to 2 days. Cover and refrigerate any leftover juices.

Tear the remaining mint leaves into a pestle and mortar, pound into a paste, then muddle and pound in around 100g of sugar so you can sprinkle it. Leave to dry out on a tray – you'll only need a pinch per person, so save the rest in an airtight jar for future meals, where it will keep happily for up to 1 month.

TO SERVE Warm through and reduce any reserved juices until jammy. Unwrap and turn out the summer pud, drizzle over the jammy syrup, then serve each lovely portion with clotted cream and a sprinkling of mint sugar.

6

LAST-MINUTE FEAST

Starter

QUICK & EASY ANTIPASTI

Main

EFFORTLESSLY ELEGANT PASTA

Pud

PANETTONE FRENCH TOAST

Peaches, melted chocolate & ice cream

Often the best get-togethers are unplanned, but if you're clever in you

approach and have a few tricks up your sleeve, deliciousness will ensue.

QUICK & EASY ANTIPASTI

TASTY & WONDERFULLY FLEXIBLE

Here, I'm sharing a whole bunch of easy cheat ideas. Pick as few or as many of these dishes as you like, to share – it's about creating contrast in colour, taste and texture, so have fun with it.

PECORINO

CHILLI JAM

— SERVES 6 —

TO SERVE Finely slice <u>6 x ½cm-thick triangles of pecorino cheese</u> and arrange on a serving board, then top each slice with <u>½ a teaspoon of quality chilli jam</u>. A simple but delicious combo. Another great pairing is nuggets of <u>Parmesan cheese</u> teamed with some thick <u>balsamic vinegar</u>. Simply pair up on a serving plate.

FIGS & HONEY

PROSCIUTTO & NUTS

— SERVES 6 —

TO SERVE Arrange <u>6 slices of prosciutto</u> in elegant waves on a serving platter, then cut <u>3 ripe figs</u> into thin wedges and arrange on top. Drizzle with <u>1 heaped teaspoon of runny honey</u>, then sprinkle with <u>2 teaspoons of bashed-up toasted hazelnuts</u> (or a nut of your choice).

DRESSED OLIVES

HAVE FUN WITH IT

— SERVES 6 —

ON THE DAY Drain <u>1 x 180g jar of mixed stone-in olives</u>. Some olives are easy to squash and destone, but the larger, firmer ones sometimes respond better to the flesh being sliced away from the stone with a small sharp knife. Either way, place the flesh in a bowl with 2 tablespoons of boiling kettle water to purge some of the salt away. Sit for 1 minute, then drain, add a splash of red wine vinegar, drizzle with 1 tablespoon of extra virgin olive oil, add a few <u>inner celery leaves</u> and toss together. From this base, you can flavour the olives any way you like – chilli, chopped anchovies, finely chopped preserved lemon, or fresh green herbs – use your imagination.

BABY MOZZARELLA

PISTACHIO, PECORINO & PARSLEY PESTO

— SERVES 6 —

TO SERVE To make the pesto, in a pestle and mortar, smash ½ **a peeled garlic clove** and a pinch of sea salt into a paste. Tear in the top leafy half of **1 bunch of flat-leaf parsley (30g)** and bash again until pulped, followed by **2 tablespoons of shelled unsalted pistachios**. Finely grate in **30g of pecorino or Parmesan cheese**, muddle in the juice of ½ **a lemon** and 2 tablespoons of extra virgin olive oil to loosen, then season to perfection, tasting and tweaking. Spoon the pesto over a serving plate. Top with **150g of baby mozzarella balls** (drained), or you could tear over a ball of buffalo mozzarella or burrata. Finish with a drizzle of extra virgin olive oil, and I like to add a few extra chopped pistachios and parsley leaves to tell the story.

BORLOTTI BEANS

ROSEMARY, GARLIC & CHILLI

— SERVES 6 —

ON THE DAY Peel and finely slice <u>2 cloves of garlic</u> and place in a non-stick pan on a medium heat with ½ a tablespoon of olive oil and <u>1 pinch of dried red chilli flakes</u>, then strip in the leaves from <u>3 sprigs of rosemary</u>. Stir regularly until lightly golden, then chop the tender heads off <u>100g of sprouting broccoli</u> (slice the stalks and use in soup or stew another day), add to the pan and fry for 3 minutes, or until tender. Tip in <u>1 x 440g jar or tin of borlotti beans</u>, juice and all, and simmer for 7 minutes, or until softened. Finish with 1 teaspoon of red wine vinegar, 1 tablespoon of extra virgin olive oil, then season to perfection, tasting and tweaking. Serve hot, at room temperature or cold.

GRIDDLED PEPPERS

BASIL & BALSAMIC

— SERVES 6 —

ON THE DAY Drain <u>1 x 460g jar of roasted red peppers</u>, slice into each so you can open them out like a book, then pat dry with kitchen paper. Char on a screaming hot griddle pan until bar-marked on one side only, then remove to a platter. Drizzle with 1 tablespoon of extra virgin olive oil and a little <u>balsamic vinegar</u>, then season with black pepper. Peel, very finely slice and scatter over <u>½ a clove of raw garlic</u>, then pick over the leaves from <u>2 sprigs of basil</u>. Serve at room temperature or cold.

DRESSED CHICKPEAS

SAGE & CHILLI

— SERVES 6 —

ON THE DAY Crush <u>2 whole unpeeled garlic cloves</u> and place in a non-stick pan on a medium-high heat with 1 tablespoon of olive oil. Pick in the leaves from <u>2 sprigs of sage</u>, then halve <u>1 fresh red chilli</u> lengthways and add. Tip in <u>1 x 660g jar of chickpeas</u>, juice and all, simmer for 10 minutes, stirring occasionally, then squeeze the soft garlic out of the skins, mash, and stir through. Season to perfection, tasting and tweaking, drizzle with 1 tablespoon of extra virgin olive oil, and serve hot, at room temperature or cold.

CREAMY BEAN DIP

PERFECT FOR DUNKING

ROSEMARY TOASTS

GARLIC & GOOD OIL

— SERVES 6 —

ON THE DAY Tip <u>1 x 600g jar of white beans</u> into a blender, juice and all, add <u>1 pinch of dried red chilli flakes</u>, 2 tablespoons of extra virgin olive oil and the juice of <u>½ a lemon</u>, then blitz until smooth. Season to perfection, tasting and tweaking, then spoon into a bowl and drizzle with a little more extra virgin olive oil. Great with cold crunchy veg, such as chicory, radishes, celery, or breadsticks, for dunking. Keep any leftovers in an airtight container in the fridge for up to 3 days.

— SERVES 6 —

TO SERVE Preheat the grill to high. Lay out <u>6 x 1cm-thick slices of sourdough bread</u> on a baking tray. Brush with <u>6 olive oil-rubbed rosemary sprigs</u>, adding them to the tray for bonus flavour. Grill until lightly golden on both sides – keep an eye on them. Rub the toasts with the cut side of <u>1 halved raw garlic clove</u> and drizzle each slice with a little extra virgin olive oil. Great on their own, as a vehicle for cheese, or for dunking.

BALSAMIC ONIONS

SWEET & STICKY

— SERVES 6 —

ON THE DAY Drain <u>1 x 400g jar of baby silverskin pickled onions</u> and tip into a non-stick pan on a high heat with ½ a tablespoon of olive oil (save the liquor in the jar and you can use it to pickle matchsticked crunchy veg, if you like). Toss together over the heat for 5 minutes, or until golden, then strip in the leaves from <u>3 sprigs of thyme</u> and add <u>2 tablespoons of balsamic vinegar</u>. Reduce to a sticky coating, and serve hot, at room temperature or cold.

DRESSED ARTICHOKES

GARLIC, CHILLI & MINT

— SERVES 6 —

ON THE DAY Drain <u>1 x 280g jar of artichoke hearts</u> (saving the oil) and chop into 1cm wedges. Peel <u>1 clove of garlic</u>, finely slice with <u>1 fresh red chilli</u>, and place both in a non-stick pan on a medium heat with ½ a tablespoon of reserved artichoke oil, tossing regularly. Pick in the leaves from <u>4 sprigs of mint</u>, and fry until everything is lightly golden and the mint is crispy. Add the artichokes, toss together over the heat for a couple of minutes, then serve on a platter – enjoy hot, at room temperature or cold.

EFFORTLESSLY ELEGANT PASTA

CHILLI, MINT, ALMONDS, DOUBLE CREAM & PARMESAN

SERVES 6

150ml double cream

50g Parmesan cheese

50g whole blanched almonds

1 clove of garlic

1 fresh red chilli

1 lemon

4 sprigs of mint

750g fresh lasagne sheets

TO SERVE Put a large pan of boiling salted water on a high heat. Pour the cream into a large serving bowl, then finely grate in the Parmesan. Pound up the almonds in a pestle and mortar until fine. Peel and pound in the garlic, finely slice and add the chilli, finely grate in the lemon zest, tear in the mint leaves and pound it all together, then squeeze in the lemon juice and muddle in 2 tablespoons of extra virgin olive oil. Spoon into the bowl with the cream, then sit it over the pan of water to gently warm through, stirring occasionally, while you use a large sharp knife to cut the lasagne sheets into ½cm strips.

Remove the bowl of sauce from the pan and cook the pasta in the boiling water for 3 minutes, or until just cooked through. Use tongs to move it straight into the sauce, letting little splashes of cooking water go with it. Toss together until you have a silky sauce, loosening with extra splashes of cooking water, if needed, then season to perfection, tasting and tweaking. Serve right away in the middle of the table, finishing with an extra drizzle of extra virgin olive oil.

PANETTONE FRENCH TOAST

PEACHES, MELTED CHOCOLATE & ICE CREAM

SERVES 6

2 x 2cm-thick round slices of
   a large panettone

1 knob of soft unsalted butter

4 large eggs

1 teaspoon vanilla bean paste

1 teaspoon icing sugar, plus
   extra for sprinkling

1 x 415g tin of peach halves
   in juice

100g quality milk or dark (70%)
   chocolate

vanilla ice cream, to serve

optional: amaretto, vin santo,
   Baileys

TO SERVE Preheat the grill to medium. Slice two thick rounds of panettone. Get a non-stick pan with the same diameter and rub the soft butter all over the base. Beat the eggs with the vanilla paste and icing sugar in a shallow bowl, then dip one of the panettone slices in the eggy mixture until well soaked on both sides. Quickly and confidently transfer to the cold buttered pan. Drain the peaches and finely slice, then lay across the eggy panettone in the pan. Snap up and scatter over the chocolate. At this point, I've been known to add a little swig of amaretto, vin santo or Baileys – it's up to you. Dip the second slice of panettone in the eggy mixture, then pour any excess egg over the chocolate and peaches. Sit the second panettone slice on top, and press down gently to compact so the egg is absorbed everywhere – don't worry if the panettone tears, just patch it up, it's all going to cook into one batch of deliciousness.

Place the pan on a medium heat for 3 minutes, to encourage a nice, crispy bottom, then sprinkle with a little extra icing sugar and pop under the grill for 10 minutes, or until the top is beautifully golden – keep an eye on it. Safely and confidently tip the panettone French toast sandwich on to a board, and sift over a final extra dusting of icing sugar from a height. Wedge it up and serve hot or warm, with scoops of vanilla ice cream. Heaven.

7

STEAK NIGHT

Starter

BLOODY MARY CRUMPETS

With smoked salmon, prawns & brown shrimp

Main

ROASTED RUMP STEAK

*Served with grilled & roasted potatoes, roasted red onions,
watercress sauce & amazing round lettuce salad*

Pud

CARAMELIZED PINEAPPLE TARTLETS

Make your menu work for you — when your best mates are coming over,

...ou want to be in the thick of it, having fun, not slaving over a hot stove.

BLOODY MARY CRUMPETS

SMOKED SALMON, PRAWNS & BROWN SHRIMP

SERVES 6

120g smoked salmon

½ a bunch of dill (10g)

300g cottage cheese

2 lemons

2 large eggs

2 tablespoons creamed
    horseradish

2 tablespoons tomato ketchup

2 teaspoons Worcestershire
    sauce

6 crumpets

1 knob of unsalted butter

150g raw shell-off prawns

smoked paprika

150g cooked brown shrimp

GET AHEAD Lay out the salmon and cut out six pretty slices that you can wrap around 6 small sprigs of dill, discarding the tougher stalks. Roll them up for a 1980's-style garnish, place on a plate, cover and return to the fridge.

Very finely chop the rest of the salmon and place in a bowl with the cottage cheese. Pick, finely chop and add most of the remaining dill, then squeeze in the juice of 1 lemon and season to perfection, tasting and tweaking. Crack the eggs into a shallow bowl and whisk with the horseradish, ketchup, Worcestershire sauce and a pinch of black pepper. Cover both and refrigerate overnight.

TO SERVE Place a large non-stick frying pan on a medium-high heat. Once hot, add 1 tablespoon of olive oil. Dunk the crumpets into the bowl of egg mixture, pressing lightly and turning to encourage them to soak up the mixture. Cook for 2 minutes on each side, or until golden (in batches, if needed). Alongside, place a medium non-stick pan on a high heat with the butter, prawns and a pinch of paprika. After a couple of minutes, add the shrimp to the prawns and toss for a minute, then squeeze in the juice of ½ a lemon and turn the heat off.

Divide the crumpets between your plates, topping with the creamy salmon mixture. Spoon over the prawns and shrimp, add the smoked salmon rolls and remaining dill, then flick over an extra pinch of paprika, if you like. Serve with lemon wedges, for squeezing over. Delicious with champagne or whisky.

ROASTED RUMP STEAK

FRAGRANT ROSEMARY & BUTTER

SERVES 6 WITH LEFTOVERS

This meal is such a fantastic reimagining of steak and chips. It allows us to truly enjoy and celebrate the rump cut as a bigger joint, and as the oven does the hard work for you, all the last-minute smoke and stress is removed from the process. This piece of steak is slightly bigger than you need, but it cooks well at this size and is worth it for the leftovers.

1.5kg piece of thick rump steak

1 bunch of rosemary (20g)

2 knobs of unsalted butter

2 tablespoons balsamic vinegar

ON THE DAY Get the meat out of the fridge an hour before you want to start cooking it, then you can do this first stage an hour or two before you roast it. Rub the steak all over with 1 tablespoon of olive oil, then sear on every side in a screaming-hot griddle pan, or on a hot barbecue, until pleasingly bar-marked. Strip half the rosemary into a roasting tray, sit the seared steak on top, strip over the rest of the rosemary, dot and rub over the butter, drizzle with another tablespoon of oil, then season generously with sea salt and black pepper.

TO SERVE Preheat the oven to 200°C. Roast the steak on the bottom of the oven for 20 minutes for medium-rare, or 25 minutes for medium, turning halfway and basting with the juices from the tray. Remove from the oven, spoon over the balsamic, then cover with tin foil and leave to rest for 15 minutes, basting occasionally – I like to slip a tea towel under one end of the tray, so the juices naturally gather at the other end and you can easily spoon off any excess fat into a clean jam jar (for the best roasties another day). Thinly slice and serve, drizzling each portion with resting juices. The leftovers will make an epic sarnie.

VEGGIE LOVE

Create a squash steak for each veggie guest – scrub 1 butternut squash (1.2kg), carefully halve lengthways and deseed, then cut a long 2cm-thick slice. Beautifully griddle twice on each side in a screaming-hot griddle pan to create criss-cross bar marks, then dress and season in exactly the same way as the steak and roast for 30 minutes, or until soft and sumptuous, basting as you go.

GRILLED & ROASTED POTATOES

LEMON, GARLIC & SAGE

SERVES 6

1 bunch of sage (20g)

1½ lemons

1 bulb of garlic

1.5kg potatoes

ON THE DAY Pick the sage leaves into your largest roasting tray, then use a speed-peeler to strip in the lemon peel, and squeeze in the juice. Drizzle in 2 tablespoons of olive oil, add a pinch of sea salt and black pepper, then break apart the unpeeled garlic bulb into the tray. Scrub the potatoes, then cut into 1cm-thick slices. Working in batches, place on a large screaming-hot griddle pan for a couple of minutes on each side, pressing them down with a fish slice until beautifully bar-marked, and transferring to the roasting tray as you go. Toss together, then spread out in a single layer. Cover until needed.

TO SERVE Preheat the oven to 200°C. Roast the potatoes, uncovered, for 45 minutes on the top shelf, or until cooked through and lightly golden. Squeeze the soft garlic cloves out of their skins, to serve.

ROASTED RED ONIONS

GARLIC, THYME, HONEY & VINEGAR

— SERVES 6 —

ON THE DAY Preheat the oven to 200°C. Peel **5 red onions**, cut into 1cm-thick rounds and place in a large roasting tray. Dot over **1 knob of unsalted butter** and drizzle with 1 tablespoon of olive oil, then peel, slice and scatter in **4 cloves of garlic**, as well as the sprigs from **½ a bunch of thyme (10g)**. Add a pinch of sea salt and black pepper, toss together, then arrange in a single layer. Roast for 30 minutes on the middle shelf, giving the tray a jiggle halfway through. Remove, drizzle with **1 tablespoon of runny honey** and 2 tablespoons of red wine vinegar, mix well and shake flat. Cover with tin foil until needed.

TO SERVE When the steak is resting (page 126), return the onions to the oven, covered, for 15 minutes, or until sticky and sweet. Before serving, season to perfection, tasting and tweaking.

WATERCRESS SAUCE

PEPPERY & VIBRANT

— SERVES 6 —

A real game-changer and a little bit different,
this sauce is so easy to make and really very good
when teamed with red meat like roasted rump.

ON THE DAY Pack <u>85g of watercress</u> into a blender, discarding the tougher stalks. Add <u>10 small silverskin pickled onions</u> and a good splash of their liquor, <u>1 tablespoon of baby capers in brine</u>, <u>2 teaspoons of English mustard</u> and <u>8 anchovy fillets in oil</u>. Remove the crusts from <u>2 thick slices of white bread (100g total)</u>, tear in the soft middles, add 3 tablespoons of extra virgin olive oil and 200ml of boiling kettle water, then blitz until silky smooth. Season to perfection, tasting and tweaking. Pour into a serving bowl, ready to serve at room temperature when your meal is ready.

AMAZING ROUND LETTUCE SALAD

YOGHURTY MUSTARD DRESSING & PARMESAN

SERVES 6

50g Parmesan cheese

½ a lemon

6 tablespoons natural yoghurt

20g feta cheese

4 anchovy fillets in oil

1 teaspoon English mustard

3 small round lettuces

ON THE DAY For the dressing, finely grate a third of the Parmesan and the lemon zest into a blender, squeeze in the juice and add the yoghurt, feta, anchovies and mustard. Blitz until smooth, then pour into a large shallow bowl. Season to perfection, tasting and tweaking. Finely grate the remaining Parmesan into another shallow bowl. Keep both in the fridge until needed.

TO SERVE Remove the outer leaves from the lettuces and save for another day, leaving you with the compact middles. Give them a wash, drain well and pat dry, then dunk each lettuce into the dressing, jiggling it about to coat. Let any excess drip off, then gently prise the leaves apart a little and turn in the bowl of Parmesan, until coated all over, and place on a platter, ready to serve.

CARAMELIZED
PINEAPPLE TARTLETS

COCONUT VANILLA SPONGE & CRISPY NUTMEG FILO

SERVES 6

2 tablespoons caster sugar

1 x 435g tin of pineapple rings in juice

20g desiccated coconut, plus extra for sprinkling

30g ground almonds

1 teaspoon vanilla bean paste

60ml semi-skimmed milk

3 sheets of filo pastry

1 whole nutmeg, for grating

6 quality jarred cherries in syrup

coconut yoghurt or vanilla ice cream, to serve

ON THE DAY Sprinkle the sugar into a large non-stick frying pan on a medium-high heat, then add the juice from the pineapple tin, along with a splash of water. Let it simmer until bubbling and the sugar has dissolved, then carefully place six pineapple rings into the pan. Cook until the syrup has reduced and the pineapple is lightly golden on each side, turning halfway and gently swirling them in the syrup occasionally, then turn the heat off and leave to cool completely.

Meanwhile, whisk the coconut, almonds, vanilla paste and milk together. Lay out one filo sheet, brush with a little olive oil and add a few scrapings of nutmeg, then repeat, stacking up all three sheets. Cut into six squares, then divide the sponge batter between them, spooning it into the centre of each and spreading it out a little. Top each with a sticky pineapple ring, gently pressing them into the batter. Casually fold the filo upwards around the pineapple (like you see in the picture), lining the tartlets up on a lightly oiled baking tray as you go. Sprinkle with a little extra desiccated coconut, then spoon over any remaining syrup from the pan. Cover, and refrigerate till needed.

TO SERVE Preheat the oven to 180°C. Bake the tartlets on the bottom of the oven for 20 minutes exactly. Serve with a cherry in the centre of each and a drizzle of cherry syrup. Finish with a dollop of yoghurt or a scoop of ice cream.

FUN FAMILY MEAL

Starter

SCRUMPTIOUS GARLIC BREAD

Main

CRISPY PESTO CHICKEN

With comforting red rice & Buddy's green salad

Pud

ESSEX ETON MESS

Jelly, meringue, yoghurt, berries, chocolate sauce & sprinkles

Feeding family can be an emotional rollercoaster. But the moments when you

...get it right, silence descends, and they ask for seconds, make it all worthwhile.

SCRUMPTIOUS GARLIC BREAD

PARSLEY, LEMON & CREAM CHEESE

SERVES 12

Who doesn't love garlic bread? And this tear and share style is always a winner. I've written the recipe for 12, because it's an easier quantity of dough to work with. What I like to do is make up both trays of bread, then whack one in the freezer, ready to bake another day – you won't regret it.

1 x 7g sachet of dried yeast

500g strong bread flour,
    plus extra for dusting

50g white or wholemeal bread

1 big bunch of flat-leaf parsley
    (60g)

3 cloves of garlic

1 lemon

200g light cream cheese

GET AHEAD You can do this on the day, if you prefer. Pour 325ml of tepid water into a large bowl. Add the yeast and mix with a fork for 2 minutes. Pour in the flour and a good pinch of sea salt, then use a fork to mix until you can't move it any more. Now, get your clean hands in there and bring it together as a ball of dough, adding more flour, if needed, to stop your hands and the dough sticking. Knead on a flour-dusted surface for 5 minutes, or until silky and elastic. Shape into a rough ball, place in a lightly oiled bowl, cover with a clean, damp tea towel, and prove in a warm place for 1 hour, or until doubled in size.

Meanwhile, tear the bread into a blender and blitz into crumbs. Rub two 20cm x 30cm trays with olive oil, then evenly scatter over the breadcrumbs. Tear the top leafy half of the parsley into the blender. Peel and add the garlic, then blitz until fine. Squeeze in the lemon juice, add the cream cheese, blitz again until smooth, then season to perfection, tasting and tweaking.

Knock the air out of the dough by punching it with your fist, then divide into two. One piece at a time, pull and stretch out on an oiled surface to 30cm x 50cm. Spread over half the cream cheese mixture, leaving a 5cm border along the longer side that's farthest away from you. Now, take your time to roll up the dough, starting in front of you, so you end up with a long Swiss roll shape. With a sharp knife, cut the roll into 18 pieces, then place in the tray, swirl-side up, arranging them fairly close together. Cover and prove in the fridge overnight (45 minutes, or until doubled in size, if making on the day).

TO SERVE Preheat the oven to 220°C. Uncover and bake on the top shelf for 20 minutes, or until golden. Drizzle with a little extra virgin olive oil, to serve.

THE FREEZER IS YOUR FRIEND

With the second tray of garlic bread, shape and prove for 45 minutes, then cover and freeze until needed. Simply bake from frozen for 25 minutes.

CRISPY PESTO CHICKEN

BREADCRUMBS & LEMON

SERVES 6

6 x 150g skinless chicken breasts

100g plain flour

3 large eggs

250g white or wholemeal bread

4 heaped teaspoons green pesto

1 lemon

GET AHEAD Use a sharp knife to carefully cut each chicken breast in half through the middle to give you two thin flat pieces (you can ask your butcher to do this for you, if you like). Sprinkle the flour into a shallow bowl or tray, then beat the eggs in another. Tear the bread into a food processor, add the pesto and 2 tablespoons of olive oil, blitz into crumbs, then tip into a tray. Now get a production line going, turning each piece of chicken in the flour until evenly coated, then dipping in the egg, letting any excess drip off. Finally turn the chicken in the pesto crumbs, taking a moment to flatten each piece on a board with your palm, pressing in the crumbs to help them stick. Stack up the coated chicken in a tray, cover and refrigerate overnight.

TO SERVE Preheat the oven to 220°C. Lay the coated chicken across two baking trays. Once the garlic bread (page 142) is cooked, bake the chicken on the top two shelves for 20 minutes, or until golden and cooked through, turning halfway. Serve with lemon wedges, for squeezing over.

VEGGIE LOVE

Swap in 1cm-thick slices of courgette, aubergine or mushroom for any veggie guests – simply flour, egg and breadcrumb before you do the chicken, and bake on a lightly oiled tray.

COMFORTING RED RICE

CARAMELIZED VEG & TOMATO SAUCE, MOZZARELLA & BASIL

SERVES 6

2 carrots

2 red onions

2 red peppers

2 cloves of garlic

2 x 400g tins of plum tomatoes

250g risotto rice

1 x 400g tin of cannellini beans

150g baby mozzarella balls

2 sprigs of basil

GET AHEAD Peel the carrots and onions, deseed the peppers, then roughly chop it all, placing in a large non-stick casserole pan on a medium heat with 1 tablespoon of olive oil. Peel and add the garlic and cook for 30 minutes, or until soft and caramelized, stirring regularly and adding splashes of water to stop it sticking, as needed. Pour the tomatoes into a food processor. Add the soft veg and blitz until super smooth, then season to perfection, tasting and tweaking. Pour the sauce back into the pan, then cool, cover and refrigerate overnight.

TO SERVE Preheat the oven to 220°C. Stir the rice and beans, juice and all, into the sauce, with 1 tin's worth of water, then place on a high heat and bring to the boil. Put the lid on and simmer for 5 minutes, then remove the lid and cook on the bottom shelf of the oven for 20 minutes, or until the rice is soft and a pleasure to eat. Quarter and dot over the baby mozzarella balls, tear over the basil leaves, add a few drips of extra virgin olive oil and serve.

BUDDY'S GREEN SALAD

LITTLE GEM, APPLE, CUCUMBER & HERBS

SERVES 6

1 lemon

1 tablespoon balsamic vinegar

1 cucumber

1 apple

2 little gem lettuces

6 green olives

1 bunch of soft herbs (30g),
    such as tarragon, chives,
    dill, mint, basil

TO SERVE Squeeze the lemon juice into a clean jam jar, add the balsamic and three times as much extra virgin olive oil, then a pinch of sea salt and black pepper, and pop the lid on. Use a speed-peeler to peel the cucumber, halve it lengthways, use a teaspoon to remove the seedy core, then slice 2cm thick, using a crinkle-cut knife, if you've got one. Chop the apple into chunky matchsticks. Trim the lettuce bases and click apart the leaves. Squash and destone the olives, tearing up the flesh. Finely chop the herb leaves. Pile it all into a large serving bowl, then give the dressing a good shake and drizzle 2 tablespoons over the salad, gently tossing it together with your fingertips. The leftover jam jar dressing will keep happily in the fridge for up to a week.

MIX IT UP

Feel free to embellish further with other gorgeous green things like chunks of ripe avocado, fresh raw peas or broad beans, speed-peeled asparagus or sliced pear.

ESSEX ETON MESS

JELLY, MERINGUE, YOGHURT, BERRIES, CHOCOLATE SAUCE & SPRINKLES

Where do I start with this one? It's delicious and fun, so embrace your inner child and celebrate a bunch of your favourite ingredients in one wonderful megamix mish-mash. I've given suggestions below, but truly the ensuing enjoyment rests on your chosen combos. Of course, fro-yo or ice cream instead of yoghurt is always going to be an added bonus.

SERVES 6

---

4 leaves of gelatine

600ml smooth unsweetened fruit juice

2 tablespoons sprinkles, such as desiccated coconut, shelled unsalted pistachios, blanched hazelnuts, mixed seeds, jarred cherries, unsalted popcorn

500g mixed seasonal fruit, such as oranges, strawberries, blueberries, raspberries

150g dark chocolate (70%)

150ml semi-skimmed milk

500g Greek-style yoghurt

6 meringues

GET AHEAD Put the gelatine into a small bowl and cover with cold water. Pour your chosen fruit juice into a small pan and place over a medium heat until almost boiling, then turn the heat off. Remove the gelatine leaves from the water and whisk into the juice until melted, then divide between moulds and bowls of your choice. Leave to cool, then cover and set in the fridge overnight. In a small non-stick pan, toast any nuts you're using until lightly golden, then decant into a cute bowl, cover and store. Prep your oranges, if using – top and tail, then, standing them on one of the flat ends, trim off the peel. Segment and place in a bowl, cover and refrigerate overnight.

TO SERVE Make a chocolate sauce by snapping the chocolate into a small non-stick pan with the milk. Place on a medium heat until smooth and combined, stirring constantly. Now you have a choice on the serving – either take everything to the table with the yoghurt and meringue and let people build their own, or smash it all up together and serve ready mixed. Have fun with it!

9

SUMMERY FEAST

Starter

RAINBOW TOMATO CROSTINI

Main

SLOW-ROASTED LAMB

*With fennel, sage, onion & merguez stuffing. Served with lemon
potatoes, dressed beans, apricot sauce & green sauce*

Pud

YOGHURT PANNA COTTA

With elderflower strawberries, mint & crushed biscuits

Oh what a joy to share delicious food and conversation with those you love

on balmy summer days. Bold, vivacious flavours and unctuous textures unite.

RAINBOW TOMATO CROSTINI

This confident little starter is one of the most honest, satisfying expressions of tomatoes. Every type has a different flavour, and some of the ugliest are the most delicious, so please be open-minded when selecting your ripe tomatoes. Buying them on the vine helps, as does letting them sunbathe on your windowsill before use.

SERVES 12

400g each of green, yellow, orange and red tomatoes (1.6kg total)

1 bunch of soft herbs (30g), such as flat-leaf parsley, basil, dill, chervil, rocket

2 rustic French baguettes (200g each)

200g Caerphilly, or crumbly goat's cheese

1–2 cloves of garlic

ON THE DAY Working one colour of tomato at a time, halve them and finely grate on a box grater, rubbing and crushing all the tomato flesh through and discarding the seeds and skins. Pour into separate bowls, season each to perfection with sea salt, and place on the table, ready to serve. Pick the herb leaves into a bowl of ice-cold water. Slice the baguettes 1cm thick, lay across large baking trays, then cover with a clean damp cloth.

TO SERVE Pop the cheese on a board, ready to slice. Drain the herbs, pat dry, then toss with ½ a tablespoon each of extra virgin olive oil and red wine vinegar, and a little pinch of seasoning. Preheat the grill to high. Uncover the bread trays and toast under the grill until golden on both sides – keep an eye on them. Halve the garlic, and rub each hot toast once with the cut side. Take everything to the table and let your guests serve themselves.

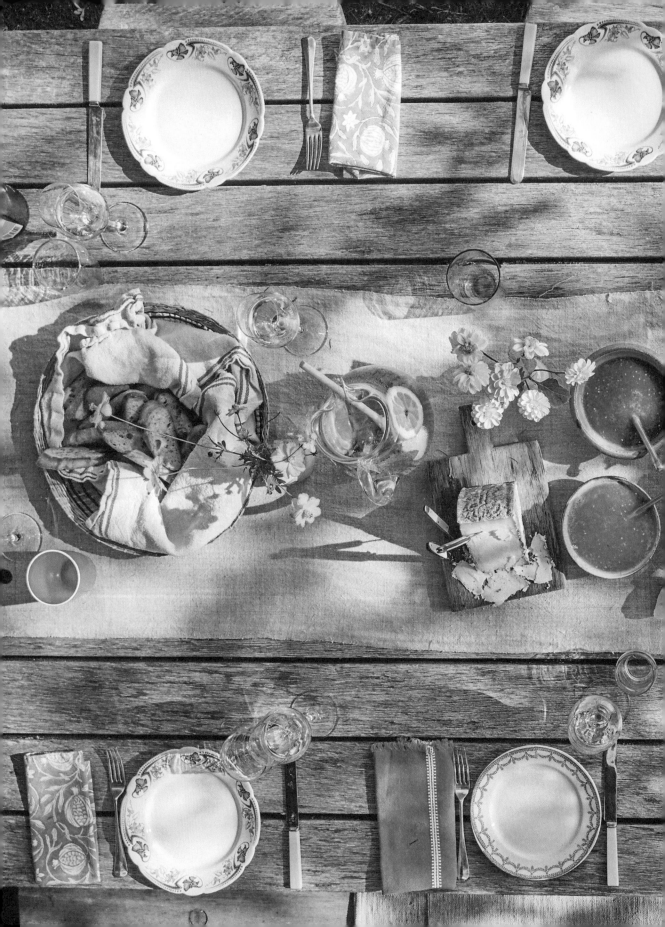

SLOW-ROASTED LAMB

FENNEL, SAGE, ONION & MERGUEZ STUFFING

Boning, stuffing and rolling the lamb means the flavourful filling infiltrates the meat as it cooks and vice versa. By stuffing the shoulder, you're able to stretch the meat even further, and by removing the bones, the lamb is easier to carve – it's a one-slice wonder!

SERVES 12 WITH LEFTOVER MEAT

5 merguez sausages
(250g total)

1 bunch of sage (20g)

2 small bulbs of fennel

2 red onions

250ml white wine

250g sourdough bread

3kg lamb shoulder, bone in
(see tip below)

1 bulb of garlic

2 heaped tablespoons plain
flour

1 tablespoon blackberry or
blackcurrant jam

GET AHEAD For the stuffing, put a high-sided roasting tray (25cm x 30cm) on a medium-high heat with 2 tablespoons of olive oil. Squeeze the sausagemeat out of the skins straight into the pan, breaking it up with the back of a spoon. Let the sausage start to crisp up, stirring occasionally, then tear in the sage leaves. Trim the fennel, peel the onions, then roughly chop both, add to the tray, and cook on a medium heat for 20 minutes, or until soft and caramelized, stirring occasionally. Pour in the wine and let it completely cook away, then season to perfection, tasting and tweaking. Chop the bread into 2cm chunks and stir in, then turn the heat off and leave to cool completely.

Lay out the lamb on a clean work surface. Scrunch and spread the cold stuffing all over the meat, then roll it up, sealing the filling inside (if any falls out, just poke it back in at the ends once tied up). Cut yourself eight 60cm lengths of string, slide them underneath the lamb at regular intervals, then tie them up at the top. Wipe out the tray, chuck in the lamb bones, break apart and add the unpeeled garlic bulb, then sit the lamb on top. Cover and refrigerate overnight.

ASK YOUR BUTCHER

To debone the lamb, then slice into it so you can open it out like a book. Get them to break up the bones, too – epic gravy, incoming!

ON THE DAY Preheat the oven to full whack (240°C). Get the lamb tray out of the fridge, rub the meat with a little olive oil, place in the oven, and turn the temperature down to 150°C. Roast for 4 hours, or until tender, basting every hour with the tray juices and adding a splash of water each time. Remove from the oven and transfer the lamb to a serving platter. Cover with tin foil and a clean tea towel, and leave to rest for 1 hour.

Use a spoon to skim the fat off the tray of bones (save it in a jar for tasty cooking another day). Put the tray over a medium heat on the hob and stir in the flour, jam and a swig of red wine vinegar, scraping up all the sticky bits from the base of the tray. Cook for a couple of minutes, then pour in 1.2 litres of water. Let it simmer on a low heat to the consistency of your liking, stirring occasionally. Pass the gravy through a sieve into a pan and season to perfection, tasting and tweaking. Simmer on the lowest heat until needed.

TO SERVE Uncover the lamb, spooning any resting juices into the gravy. Cut away the string, then spoon over the Green sauce (page 167). Take it to the table, ready to carve in front of your guests.

LEMON POTATOES

GOLDEN & CRISP

— SERVES 12 —

GET AHEAD Scrub <u>2.5kg of potatoes</u>, chop into 3cm chunks, and parboil in a large pan of boiling salted water for 10 minutes. Drain and leave to steam dry for 2 minutes, while you use a speed-peeler to strip the peel off <u>2 lemons</u>. In your largest roasting tray, toss the potatoes with the lemon peel and juice, 2 tablespoons of olive oil and a pinch of sea salt and black pepper. Cool, cover and refrigerate overnight.

TO SERVE Once the lamb (page 164) is resting, turn the oven up to 200°C. Roast the potatoes for 1 hour, or until beautifully golden and crisp, tossing gently halfway through.

DRESSED BEANS

GARLIC & VINEGAR

— SERVES 12 —

GET AHEAD Prep <u>1.2kg of mixed green and runner beans</u>. Peel <u>2 cloves of garlic</u> and finely grate into a little jug, add 2 tablespoons each of extra virgin olive oil and red wine vinegar, and a pinch of sea salt and black pepper, then mix well. Cover everything and store overnight.

TO SERVE Cook the beans in a large pan of boiling water for 7 minutes, or until just soft. Drain well, then return to the pan and toss with the dressing. Serve hot or at room temperature.

APRICOT SAUCE

INFUSED WITH THYME

— SERVES 12 —

GET AHEAD Put ½ a bunch of thyme (10g) into a mug and cover with 150ml of boiling kettle water, discarding the thyme after 1 minute. Put 125g of dried apricots into a blender. Halve, deseed and add ½ a small fresh red chilli, drizzle in 2 tablespoons of extra virgin olive oil and add a pinch of sea salt. Pour the thyme-infused water into the blender, and blitz until super-smooth. Decant into a nice serving bowl, cool, cover and refrigerate overnight.

GREEN SAUCE

PISTACHIOS, MINT & PARSLEY

— SERVES 12 —

ON THE DAY On a large board, use a large sharp knife to finely chop 1 heaped tablespoon of shelled unsalted pistachios, then squash, destone and add 1 heaped tablespoon of mixed-colour olives, as well as 1 heaped tablespoon each of baby capers in brine and baby cornichons. Add 4 anchovy fillets in oil and 2 teaspoons of English mustard, then pick over the leaves from 1 bunch each of mint and flat-leaf parsley (60g total). Chop everything until fine, mixing as you go. Scrape into a serving bowl, add 2 tablespoons of red wine vinegar, 4 tablespoons of extra virgin olive oil and just enough boiling kettle water to loosen, mix well, then season to perfection with black pepper.

YOGHURT PANNA COTTA

ELDERFLOWER STRAWBERRIES, MINT & CRUSHED BISCUITS

I love a good panna cotta. These are so utterly easy to make and great for a party. The blend of cream and yoghurt means they're fresh and elegant, and with the combination of delicate fruit and crunchy biscuits to dip each spoonful into, every mouthful is absolute bliss.

SERVES 12

3 leaves of gelatine

400ml single cream

100g golden caster sugar

2 teaspoons vanilla bean paste

400g Greek-style yoghurt

400g strawberries

4 tablespoons elderflower cordial

2 sprigs of mint

shortbread or ginger nut biscuits, to serve

GET AHEAD Put the gelatine into a small bowl and cover with cold water. Pour the cream into a pan with the sugar and vanilla paste. Place on a medium-low heat until the mixture just starts to bubble, then turn the heat off. Remove the gelatine leaves from the water and whisk into the pan until melted, followed by the yoghurt. Once smooth and combined, divide between espresso cups, small glasses or moulds, place on a tray lined with kitchen paper (to prevent them sliding about), cool, cover and leave to set in the fridge overnight.

ON THE DAY Hull and halve or quarter the strawberries, depending on their size. Mix with the cordial in a nice bowl and leave to macerate for an hour or so.

TO SERVE Either serve the panna cotta in their cups, glasses or moulds, or turn them out on to little plates or saucers – the easiest way to do this is by carefully dipping each cup into a bowl of boiling kettle water for 20 seconds, or until you get a wiggle, then place a plate on top and confidently flip out. Spoon over some strawberries and syrup, pick over a couple of cute baby mint leaves and tuck in. Delicious with a crumbling of bashed-up biscuits on the side.

10

GARDEN
LUNCH

Nibble

WATERMELON SKEWERS

With cucumber, feta, parsley & ham

Main

DUKKAH ROAST CHICKEN

*Served with warm pomegranate gravy dressing, roasted squash,
smashed aubergine & crispy chickpea rice*

Pud

APPLE & BRAMBLE CRUMBLE TART

Eating outside gives us space to reimagine some of our loyal dishes with

punchy optimism, and exciting pops of flavour that everyone will love.

WATERMELON SKEWERS

CUCUMBER, FETA, PARSLEY & HAM

It's always nice to welcome friends with something tasty and mouthwatering that pairs perfectly with a cold drink. For me, this combo is absolutely delicious, particularly on a warm day. Take pride in putting them together and get prepped ahead of time – they'll go down a treat.

SERVES 6

¼ of a small watermelon (500g)

½ a cucumber

120g feta cheese

½ a small red onion

1 lemon

½ a bunch of flat-leaf parsley (15g)

optional: serrano ham or pata negra

ON THE DAY Peel the watermelon and slice 1.5cm thick, then into 1.5cm chunks. Quarter the cucumber lengthways and chop into the same sized chunks, along with the feta. Peel and finely chop the onion and toss with the lemon juice and a pinch of sea salt and black pepper in a shallow bowl. Pick in the parsley leaves, add the cucumber, watermelon and feta and gently toss together. Spend a bit of time skewering everything up on cocktail sticks, then line up on a platter. Spoon over the juices, and pop into the fridge until needed.

TO SERVE Delicious fridge cold, with some good ham on the side.

DUKKAH ROAST CHICKEN

WARM POMEGRANATE GRAVY DRESSING

SERVES 6

1 x 350g jar of small
    preserved lemons

1 fresh red chilli

1 bunch of rosemary (20g)

1 pomegranate

1 x 1.5kg whole chicken

1 tablespoon runny honey

3 tablespoons dukkah
    (page 181)

140g wild rocket

ON THE DAY I like to time this so the chicken is coming out of the oven to rest just as my guests arrive. Preheat the oven to 180°C. Get a roasting tray that will fit the chicken fairly snugly. Halve, deseed and finely chop 4 preserved lemons and place in the tray. Roughly chop and add the chilli, strip in the rosemary, then halve the pomegranate and squeeze all the juice through your fingers into the tray. Add 1 tablespoon of olive oil, then the chicken, season lightly and rub all that flavour over the bird, getting into all the nooks and crannies.

Pour 150ml of water into the tray around the chicken and roast for 1 hour 20 minutes, or until golden and cooked through, basting halfway with the tray juices. Remove, cover and leave to rest for 30 minutes in the tray.

TO SERVE Move the chicken to a serving platter, drizzle and brush with the honey, scatter over the dukkah, then spoon the Smashed aubergine (page 180) around it. For the dressing, skim off and discard a spoonful of fat from the tray, then place the tray over a medium heat on the hob, add 1 tablespoon of red wine vinegar and simmer until thickened, scraping up all the sticky bits and loosening with splashes of water, if needed. Pour through a sieve into a little jug. Serve with the chicken, Roasted squash (page 180) and a bowl of rocket.

VEGGIE LOVE

Use 1 cauliflower (800g) instead of chicken for veggie guests – use just 2 preserved lemons in the marinade, then roast and finish it in exactly the same way as the chicken.

PRESERVE THOSE LEMONS

Preserved lemons don't last that long once the jar's open, so what I do is pour all their liquor into a blender, deseed and add the lemons, then blitz until smooth. Freeze in ice cube trays ready to jazz up stews, salads, couscous, rice, roasts and dressings.

ROASTED SQUASH

CHILLI & SAGE

— SERVES 6 —

GET AHEAD Scrub <u>1 butternut squash (1.2kg)</u> (there's no need to peel it), then carefully halve lengthways and scrape the seeds into a large roasting tray. Chop each half into 4cm chunks and add to the tray, season with sea salt and black pepper, add <u>1–2 fresh red chillies</u>, pick in the leaves from <u>½ a bunch of sage (10g)</u>, drizzle with 1 tablespoon of olive oil and toss together well. Cover and store overnight.

ON THE DAY Preheat the oven to 180°C. Roast alongside the chicken (page 176) for 1 hour 20 minutes, or until soft and golden.

SMASHED AUBERGINE

TAHINI, GARLIC & LEMON

— SERVES 6 —

ON THE DAY Preheat the oven to 180°C. Before you cook the chicken (page 176), prick <u>3 aubergines (250g each)</u>, place in a tray with <u>1 bulb of garlic</u>, and roast for 1 hour 20 minutes, or until soft. Remove and leave to cool.

Squeeze the soft garlic flesh out of the skins into the tray. Halve the aubergines lengthways, scoop out the middles, discarding the skin, then squash and break up the flesh with a fork. Add <u>2 tablespoons of tahini</u>, squeeze in the juice of <u>1 lemon</u>, finely chop and add the leaves from <u>½ a bunch of flat-leaf parsley (15g)</u>, drizzle with 1 tablespoon of extra virgin olive oil, season to perfection, tasting and tweaking, and mix well.

AMAZING DUKKAH

TOASTED NUTS & SEEDS, LEMON & SPICE

— MAKES 1 SMALL JAR —

An Egyptian mix of toasted nuts, seeds and spices,
use dukkah over flatbreads, in salads and stews, or
sprinkled on to roasted or grilled meat and veg.

GET AHEAD In a non-stick frying pan on a medium heat, toast <u>1 tablespoon</u> <u>each of black peppercorns, sea salt, coriander seeds and fennel seeds</u> with <u>1 teaspoon of cumin seeds</u> and the finely grated zest of <u>1 lemon</u> for 4 minutes, then tip into a large pestle and mortar. Pound until fine while you toast <u>50g each of blanched almonds and hazelnuts</u> in the hot pan for 2 minutes, adding <u>50g of sesame seeds</u> for a final minute. Tip it all into the mortar and pound into the mix with <u>50g of shelled unsalted pistachios</u>. Cool, then decant into an airtight jar and store until needed – it'll keep happily for weeks!

CRISPY CHICKPEA RICE

LEMON & SOFT FRAGRANT HERBS

Good rice dishes are a great thing to have up your sleeve. Inspired by Persian rice dishes I've had the pleasure of eating in the past, this recipe gives you both crispy and fluffy textures, as well as the fragrance of fresh herbs. Take this method as a principle you can enjoy in different ways.

SERVES 6

300g basmati rice

½ a lemon

1 bunch of mixed mint, dill & flat-leaf parsley (30g)

1 x 400g tin of chickpeas

GET AHEAD You can make this on the day, if you prefer. Put the rice into a pan, cover with boiling kettle water and boil for 6 minutes, then cool quickly under cold running water and drain well. Transfer to a bowl, toss with a pinch of sea salt and the lemon juice, then remove one third to a cold 24cm non-stick frying pan and toss with 1 tablespoon of olive oil. Spread it across the base of the pan. Finely chop the herb leaves and toss through half the remaining rice in one side of the bowl, then pile into the pan. Drain the chickpeas and mix into the rest of the rice, then add that to the pan, too, using your hands to shape the rice into a dome. Use the handle of a wooden spoon to poke a few holes deep into the dome, to help the rice steam and create vessels for dressing later, then cover carefully with a scrunched-up sheet of damp greaseproof paper. Use tin foil to tightly seal the pan, and refrigerate overnight.

TO SERVE When the chicken comes out, place the covered pan on a low heat to cook for 30 minutes, or until the base is golden and crispy and the rice is fluffy and hot through. Drizzle some warm pomegranate gravy dressing (page 176) into the holes, then carefully and confidently turn out on to a serving plate.

APPLE & BRAMBLE CRUMBLE TART

Apples and blackberries are often at their best at the same time of year, and they're a winning combination. In my indecision over making a pie or a crumble, I got excited and figured why not have both? So here you go! Using golden syrup gives you a flapjacky flavour kiss and, if you want to go the extra mile, the hibiscus syrup adds a delicious curiosity into proceedings, especially when drizzled hot over good ice cream.

1.2kg eating apples

150g golden syrup

300g blackberries

400g plain flour, plus
extra for dusting

75g icing sugar

1 lemon

200g cold unsalted butter,
plus extra for greasing

2 heaped tablespoons
porridge oats

2 heaped tablespoons
flaked almonds

2 sprigs of thyme

2 large eggs

vanilla ice cream, to serve

GET AHEAD Peel, core and roughly chop the apples. Put a large non-stick pan on a medium heat with 120g of golden syrup. Add the apples and cook for 20 minutes, or until soft, stirring occasionally and adding splashes of water, as needed. Toss in the blackberries for just the last couple of minutes, then turn the heat off and leave to cool.

Mix the flour and icing sugar in a large bowl, then finely grate in the lemon zest. Chop the butter into cubes, then rub in with your fingertips until the mixture resembles breadcrumbs. Remove one quarter of the mixture (about 2 big handfuls) to a separate bowl and use your fingertips to rub and mix with the oats, almonds, the remaining golden syrup and the thyme leaves. Back to the main bowl, beat and stir in 1 egg and 1 yolk (reserving the white), then gently scrunch the dough into a ball – be careful not to overwork it, we want the pastry to be crumbly and short. Wrap and rest in the freezer for 30 minutes.

Grease a deep 25cm non-stick loose-bottomed tart tin, then coarsely grate in the pastry. Use your fingertips to press it into the base and up the sides in a rustic but fairly even layer, letting it bulge up a bit at the brow of the tin, then brush with the reserved egg white. Cover everything and refrigerate overnight.

TO SERVE Preheat the oven to 180°C. Spoon the fruit into the pastry case and scatter over the crumble topping, leaving a little border at the edges. Bake on the bottom of the oven for 1 hour, or until golden and bubbling, then let it sit in the tin until you're ready to serve. Enjoy warm, with vanilla ice cream and hibiscus syrup (see below), if making – reheat for maximum enjoyment.

OPTIONAL: HIBISCUS SYRUP

Simmer 20g of dried hibiscus flowers and 40g of golden caster sugar in a small pan on a medium-low heat with 300ml of water, until syrupy, then sieve.

11

COLOURFUL COMFORT

Main

EXTRAORDINARY SEAFOOD PARCELS

Served with tender sticky aubergines,
noodle rice cake & rainbow slaw

Pud

SILKY WHITE CHOCOLATE MOUSSE

Graceful cooking can really rock your world. Here we celebrate some of th

exciting, long, vibrant flavours of Southeast Asia, with a rainbow of colour.

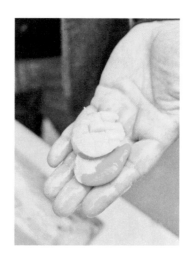

EXTRAORDINARY SEAFOOD PARCELS

FISH, SCALLOPS, KING PRAWNS, PAK CHOI & FRAGRANT GREEN SAUCE

SERVES 4

For me, recipes like this feel like a little adventure.
Sourcing beautiful fresh fish and seafood, and cooking
it all in a sealed bag really amplifies the flavours and
feels exciting, meaning each of your guests ends up
with their own parcel of treasure to enjoy.

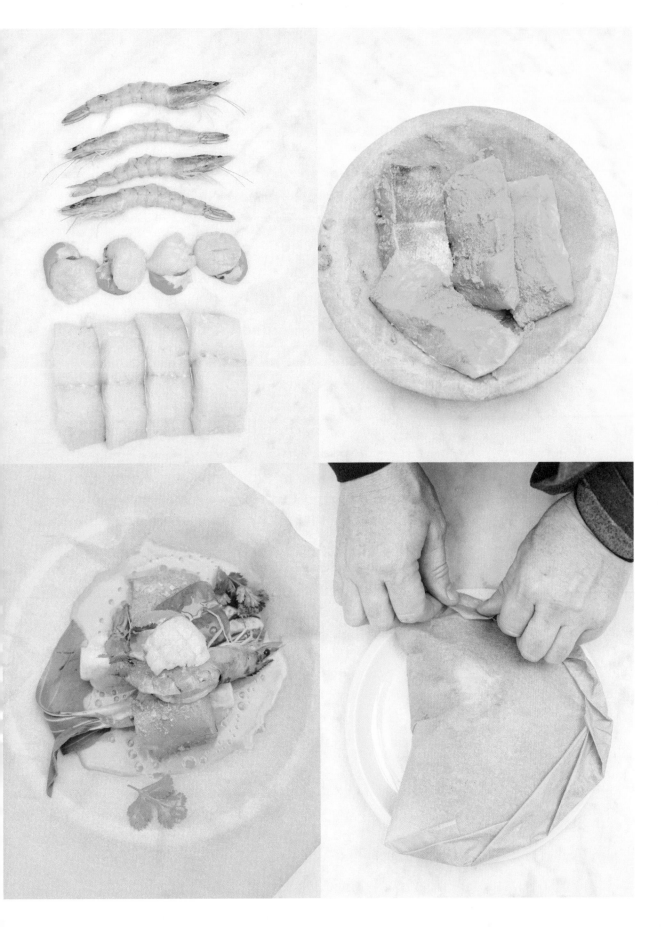

2 cloves of garlic

8cm piece of ginger

1 teaspoon ground turmeric

4 x 125g white fish fillets, skin
on, scaled, pin-boned

1 stick of lemongrass

2 spring onions

1 fresh green chilli

2 teaspoons sesame oil

3 tablespoons low-salt
soy sauce

2 limes

6 lime leaves

1 bunch of coriander (30g)

1 x 400g tin of light coconut
milk

4 raw king scallops, coral
attached, trimmed

4 large raw shell-on king
prawns

2 pak choi

1 large egg

GET AHEAD Peel the garlic and ginger. Put 1 clove into a pestle and mortar, then slice and add half the ginger, the turmeric and a small pinch of sea salt. Pound into a paste, brush all over the fish fillets, cover and refrigerate overnight.

Crush the lemongrass, remove the outer layer and trim with the spring onions. Deseed the chilli. Roughly chop it all with the remaining garlic and ginger and place in a blender with the sesame oil, soy sauce, and the lime zest. Tear in 2 lime leaves, discarding the stalks, add the coriander, stalks and all, then tip in the coconut milk. Blitz until super-smooth, and refrigerate overnight.

ON THE DAY Use a small knife to gently score a criss-cross pattern into each scallop. Leaving the heads and tails attached, remove the prawn shells, then run a knife down their backs to butterfly them, removing the vein. Quarter the pak choi lengthways. Get yourself four 50cm square sheets of greaseproof paper or tin foil, fold each in half and place a plate under half of one sheet to act as a base. Pour a quarter of the sauce into the centre – the plate will stop it running away. Sit two quarters of pak choi, one piece of fish, one prawn, one scallop and one lime leaf on top, drizzle with a tiny bit of olive oil, then eggwash the exposed paper. Fold it over, then work your way around from one side to the other, folding in as you go to seal the parcel. Carefully transfer to your largest baking tray, and repeat with the remaining ingredients.

TO SERVE Preheat the oven to 180°C. Put the tray of parcels over a high heat on the hob for 3 minutes, or until you can hear them start to sizzle, then carefully transfer to the oven for 15 minutes. Slide a parcel on to each of four plates, and let your guests tear them open at the table. Serve with lime wedges, ready to tweak the sauce to perfection.

> **VEGAN LOVE**
>
> Swap out the seafood in each parcel for 2 rounded scoops of silken tofu (125g) and 60g of shiitake or oyster mushrooms. Tinned water chestnuts would also be a joy. Replace the eggwash, too, and use a little oil instead.

TENDER STICKY AUBERGINES

STAR ANISE, CHILLI JAM & SESAME SEEDS

SERVES 4

2 large aubergines (400g each)

2 star anise

2 teaspoons sesame seeds

2 tablespoons chilli jam

2 tablespoons rice wine vinegar

2 teaspoons low-salt soy sauce

ON THE DAY Put a large non-stick frying pan on a medium-high heat. Halve the aubergines lengthways, score into the flesh in a criss-cross pattern at 2cm intervals, then sprinkle with a little sea salt. Place skin side down in the pan with ½ a tablespoon of olive oil and 2 mugs of water (600ml). Add the star anise, sesame seeds, chilli jam, vinegar and soy, then cover and boil gently for 20 to 30 minutes, or until all the water has cooked away, the aubergine is soft through, and the chilli jam is getting sticky. Turn the heat off.

TO SERVE Reheat the aubergines for 5 minutes on a medium-high heat, adding extra splashes of water to create a sticky sauce, if needed. Transfer to a serving plate but don't touch it straight away – the chilli jam means it'll be very hot!

NOODLE RICE CAKE

CRISPY & FLUFFY WITH LEMON & SESAME OIL

— SERVES 4 —

GET AHEAD You can make this on the day, if you prefer. Put <u>200g of jasmine rice</u> into a pan, cover with boiling kettle water and cook for 8 minutes. In a heatproof bowl, snap up <u>100g of vermicelli rice noodles</u>, then cover with boiling kettle water. Quickly cool the rice and noodles under cold running water and drain well. Mix well with the zest and juice of <u>1 lemon</u>, <u>1 tablespoon of sesame oil</u> and a pinch of sea salt, then beat in <u>1 large egg</u>. Rub the inside of a 20cm non-stick pan with oil, evenly pack in the mixture, cover tightly with tin foil and refrigerate overnight.

TO SERVE Place the covered pan on a low heat to cook for 25 minutes, or until the base is lightly golden and crispy and the rice is fluffy and hot through. Carefully and confidently turn out on to a serving plate.

VEGAN LOVE

Replace the egg with 2 tablespoons of dairy-free yoghurt.

RAINBOW SLAW

CRUNCHY VEG, MANGO, MINT & MAGIC DRESSING

— SERVES 4 —

ON THE DAY Peel ½ a clove of garlic, then place in a blender with **1 fresh bird's-eye chilli**, most of the leaves from **½ a bunch of mint (15g)**, **2 tablespoons of crunchy peanut butter**, **2 teaspoons each of runny honey and fish sauce**, and the juice of **4 limes**. Blitz until smooth, cover and refrigerate. Prep **500g of mixed crunchy veg, such as white cabbage, Chinese cabbage, carrots, radishes, cucumber or sugar snap peas** ready to grate later, along with **1 small mango**.

TO SERVE Coarsely grate all the veg and the mango on a box grater, or finely slice by hand, transferring them to a large serving bowl as you go. Pour over the dressing and toss together well, then pick over the remaining mint leaves.

VEGAN LOVE

Use maple syrup in place of the honey, and low-salt soy instead of the fish sauce.

SILKY WHITE CHOCOLATE MOUSSE

VANILLA, PASSION FRUIT & LIME

SERVES 4

150g white chocolate, plus
extra to serve

500g silken tofu

1 tablespoon runny honey

1 tablespoon vanilla bean paste

1 lime

4 passion fruit

GET AHEAD Melt the chocolate in a heatproof bowl over a pan of gently simmering water, making sure the water doesn't touch the base of the bowl. Line another bowl with a clean tea towel. Add the tofu, bunch up the tea towel and squeeze out as much excess moisture as possible into the bowl. Place the tofu in a food processor with the honey and vanilla paste, finely grate in the zest of just ½ a lime, then blitz for 2 minutes, or until smooth. Add the melted chocolate and blitz again until silky and combined. Pour the mixture into a nice serving bowl, cover, and refrigerate overnight.

TO SERVE Get a cup of boiling water, then dip and use a large spoon to scoop out beautiful portions of mousse on to delicate plates. Halve and spoon over the passion fruit, and finish each portion with a drizzle of melted white chocolate, or gratings or scrapings of it.

VEGAN LOVE

Simply swap in dairy-free white chocolate,
and use maple syrup instead of the honey.

12

PICNIC LOVE

To share

QUICHE

JAM JAR PRAWN COCKTAILS

GREENHOUSE COUSCOUS SALAD

PRETTY PICKLED VEG

SAVOURY SEEDED CRACKERS

Pud

TANGERINE DREAM CAKE

Picnics have always excited me. Getting outside, finding a shaded corner,

unleashing love, care and surprise, played out through food — heaven.

QUICHE

THE PRINCIPLE FOR AN EASY VEG TART

There's something so satisfying about a homemade quiche and this method guarantees delicious flavour. I like to have a pastry case ready rolled and in the freezer, waiting to blind bake when needed – the quantities I've given here are easy to double up, if you want to make an extra case and stash it away for your next picnic.

250g plain flour, plus
    extra for dusting

125g cold unsalted butter

800g butternut squash
    or mixed mushrooms

1 onion

4 cloves of garlic

6 large eggs

100ml single cream

100g Cheddar cheese

50g crumbly goat's cheese

2 sprigs of thyme

GET AHEAD You can make this all on the day, if you prefer. Equally, you can cook the whole thing the night before, and enjoy cold. Whatever works for you! Put the flour, butter and a pinch of sea salt into a food processor and pulse for 15 seconds, until the mixture resembles breadcrumbs. Add 4 tablespoons of water and pulse for a few more seconds until it comes together. Scoop on to a flour-dusted work surface and push and pat into a round – don't be tempted to knead it. Wrap and rest in the fridge for 30 minutes.

Preheat the oven to 180°C. Lightly oil a non-stick loose-bottomed tart tin (25cm diameter, 4cm deep). Roll out the pastry on a flour-dusted surface, turning it every so often, until it's just under ½cm thick. Gently roll it up around the rolling pin, then unroll it over the oiled tin and ease it into the sides, letting the excess pastry overhang. Prick the base all over with a fork, place on a baking tray, then bake blind for 30 minutes, or until lightly golden. Cool, trim off the excess pastry, and store in an airtight container.

Prep your chosen veg – peel, carefully halve and deseed the squash, then dice into 2cm chunks, or clean and slice the mushrooms. Put a large non-stick frying pan on a medium heat. Peel and finely slice the onion and garlic, then place in the pan with 1 tablespoon of olive oil. Add your chosen veg and cook for 30 minutes, or until soft and starting to caramelize, stirring occasionally and adding splashes of water to prevent it sticking, if needed. Season to perfection, then leave to cool. Tip into a blender, crack in the eggs, add the cream and grate in the Cheddar, then blitz until smooth, cover and refrigerate overnight.

ON THE DAY Preheat the oven to 180°C. Pour the filling into the pastry case, then crumble over the goat's cheese. Rub the thyme sprigs with a little oil, then pick the tips and leaves over the tart. Bake for 40 minutes exactly, then remove and leave to cool, ready to wrap and go.

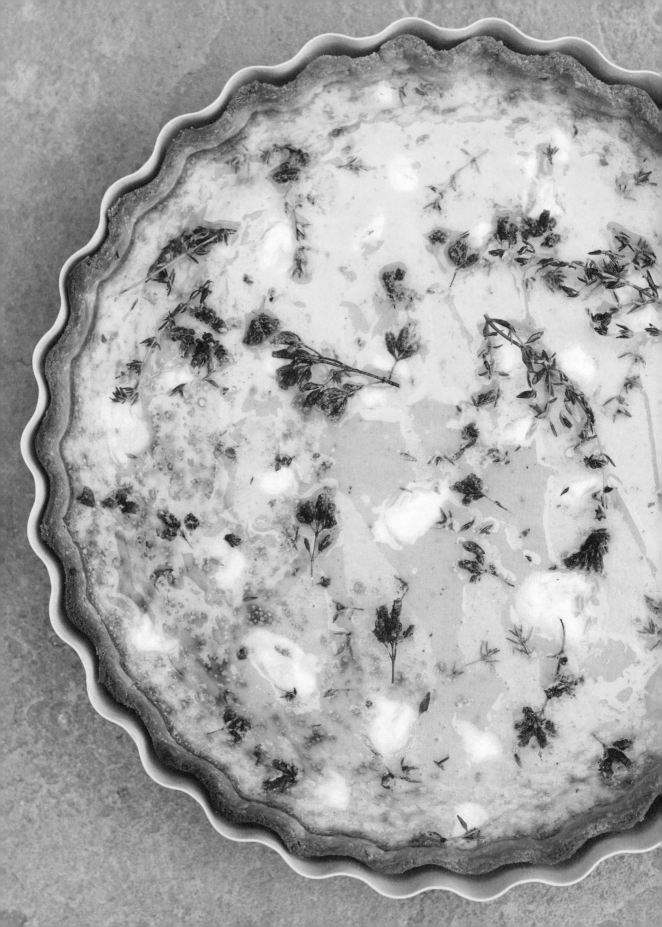

JAM JAR PRAWN COCKTAILS

COCKTAIL SAUCE, AVO, TOMATOES & CRISPY PANCETTA CRUMBS

SERVES 6

1 clove of garlic

4 rashers of smoked pancetta

100g breadcrumbs

3 tablespoons mayonnaise

3 tablespoons natural yoghurt

3 tablespoons tomato ketchup

1 lemon

Worcestershire sauce

Tabasco sauce

2 little gem lettuces

1 cucumber

200g ripe cherry tomatoes

1 punnet of cress

1 ripe avocado

100g cooked brown shrimp

200g cooked peeled prawns

cayenne pepper

ON THE DAY Peel the garlic and finely chop with the pancetta, then place in a non-stick frying pan on a medium heat with 1 teaspoon of olive oil. Add the breadcrumbs and fry until crunchy and golden, tossing regularly. Leave to cool.

For the sauce, whisk up the mayo, yoghurt, ketchup, half the lemon juice and a dash each of Worcestershire and Tabasco sauce, then season to perfection, tasting and tweaking. Finely shred the lettuces. Halve the cucumber lengthways and scrape out the seeds with a teaspoon, then chop into 1cm dice. Quarter the cherry tomatoes. Snip the cress. Halve and destone the avocado, squeeze the flesh into a blender with the remaining lemon juice and blitz until smooth, loosening with a splash of water, if needed, then season to perfection.

Line up six clean wide-necked jam jars or glasses ready to fill. Divide the lettuce between them, followed by the cucumber and tomatoes, gently pressing down as you build the layers. Spoon in the cool, crispy pancetta crumbs, top with the cress, then sprinkle in the shrimp and prawns. Drizzle in the sauce and add a pinch of cayenne to each. Spoon over the blitzed avo, cover and you're done.

PERFECT PRAWNS

A good fishmonger will have a nice selection of prawns – I like to use a mixture here, even a few smoked ones would be great. Have fun with it.

GREENHOUSE COUSCOUS SALAD

GARLICKY ROASTED COURGETTES, FETA & CHILLI

SERVES 10

700g ripe mixed-colour tomatoes

2 fresh mixed-colour chillies

1 bunch of basil (30g)

1 mug of couscous (300g)

500g baby courgettes

4 cloves of garlic

6 black olives, stone in

200g feta cheese

ON THE DAY Roughly chop the tomatoes and place in a blender with ½ a chilli. Tear in the basil, reserving a handful of nice baby leaves. Add 4 tablespoons of red wine vinegar, 2 tablespoons of water and a pinch of sea salt, then blitz until smooth (work in batches, if needed). Pour the mixture through a coarse sieve into a deep enamel tray or bowl. Season to perfection, tasting and tweaking, then stir in the couscous, cover, and leave to rehydrate in the fridge for 1 hour.

Meanwhile, preheat the oven to 180°C. Trim the baby courgettes and halve lengthways, placing them in a baking tray as you go. Peel the garlic, slice with the remaining chillies and add to the tray, then squash, destone and tear in the olives. Drizzle with 1 tablespoon of olive oil, lightly season and toss together. Rub the feta with a little oil, then place in the centre of the tray and roast for 30 minutes, or until everything is lightly golden. Mix up the couscous, scatter over the courgettes, garlic, chilli and olives, crumble over the feta, sprinkle with the reserved basil leaves, and drizzle with 1 tablespoon of extra virgin olive oil. This will be delicious served warm or cold.

PRETTY PICKLED VEG

1.2kg crunchy veg, such as fennel, carrots, celery, radishes, cauliflower, candied beets

4 fresh bay leaves

1 tablespoon mustard seeds

1 tablespoon black peppercorns

2 fresh mixed-colour chillies

350ml cider vinegar

1 tablespoon runny honey

GET AHEAD It's nice to make this a few days ahead. Get a large pan of boiling salted water on the go. Prep your veg, trimming as appropriate, then chop into bite-sized pieces that'll be a pleasure to eat, and boil for 4 minutes exactly.

Meanwhile, put the bay leaves, mustard seeds and peppercorns into a large bowl with 1 tablespoon of sea salt. Roughly slice and add the chillies, then cover with the vinegar. Add 500ml of hot liquor from the pan, then use a slotted spoon to add the veg to the bowl. Add the honey, stir well, topping up with more hot liquor to cover the veg, if needed, then sit a plate on top to keep the veg submerged. Leave to cool, then store in the fridge overnight.

The next day, divide the veg and liquor between airtight jars – I usually go for 2 x 1-litre jars, but you can absolutely use a few smaller jars, if you prefer. Seal them up, and store in the fridge until ready for your picnic, where they'll keep really well for 2 to 3 weeks. Perfect paired with good cheese and crackers, mixed into salads, added to sandwiches, or just enjoyed on their own.

SAVOURY
SEEDED CRACKERS

Crunchy and snappy, these crackers are fantastic with a wedge of cheese and some of my Pretty pickled veg (page 218), they pair perfectly with pâté, and can even be used with dips for dunking. They're fun to make, and you can lace them with different toppings, if you wish.

SERVES 10

250g plain flour

2 tablespoons rapeseed oil

4 tablespoons small mixed
seeds, such as linseed,
sesame, poppy, chia

ON THE DAY Put the flour and rapeseed oil into a bowl with a pinch of sea salt, add 125ml of water, and mix into a dough. Knead for 2 minutes, then rub the dough with oil, cover, and leave to rest for 30 minutes.

Preheat the oven to 180°C. With oiled hands, halve the dough, then press, flatten and stretch out each piece on to large oiled trays until super-thin, patching up any tears as you go. Evenly divide and scatter over all the seeds, with a pinch of sea salt. Pat the seeds in really well, then bake for 25 minutes, or until golden and crisp. Once cool, snap and wrap, ready to go. They're exceptional on the day you make them, but I enjoy them for a few days afterwards, too – keep them in an airtight tin, ready to tuck into.

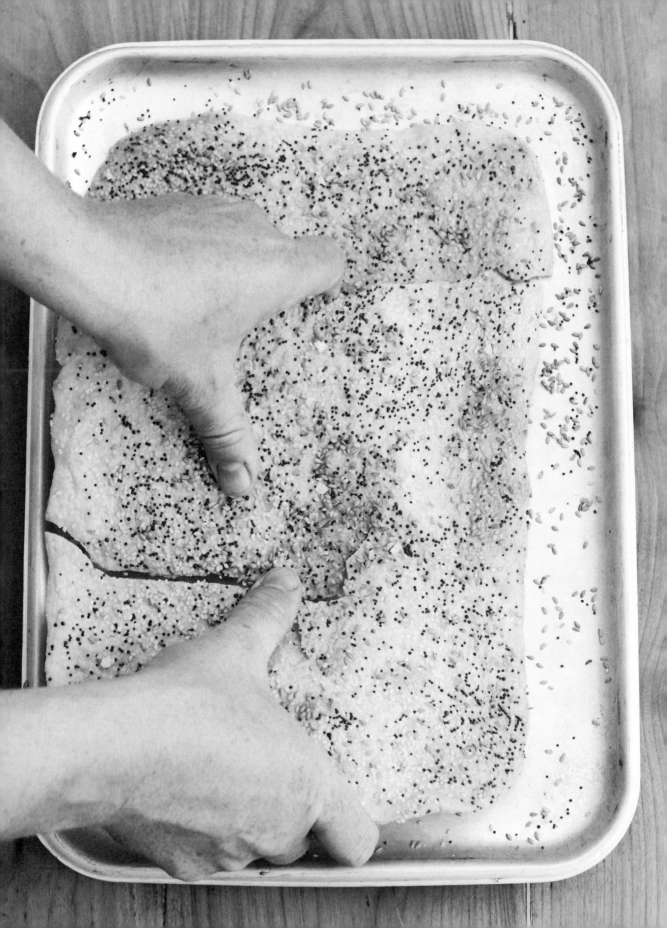

TANGERINE DREAM CAKE

A pleasure to make, this cake is joyous served with a cup of tea — make sure you pack your flask. Any leftovers crumbled over ice cream will also be a treat. I like to make the whole thing on the day, but you can absolutely make the sponge ahead and simply store it in an airtight container overnight.

SERVES 16

250g soft unsalted butter

250g runny honey

250g self-raising flour

200g ground almonds

1 tablespoon vanilla bean paste

6 large eggs

4 tangerines

100g icing sugar

optional: natural yoghurt, to serve

ON THE DAY Preheat the oven to 180°C and generously grease a 2-litre non-stick bundt tin with butter. Place the remaining butter in a food processor with the honey, flour, almonds, vanilla paste and a pinch of sea salt. Crack in the eggs, finely grate in the tangerine zest (reserving some for garnish) and blitz until smooth. Pour the mixture into the bundt tin, scraping it out of the processor with a spatula, then jiggle the tin to level it out. Bake for 30 to 35 minutes, or until golden and an inserted skewer comes out clean. Leave for a few minutes, then turn out on to a wire rack and leave to cool completely.

Sift the icing sugar into a bowl, then squeeze and stir in enough tangerine juice to make a thick drizzle. Pour or spoon over the cool cake, easing some drips down the sides in an arty way, then sprinkle over the reserved zest. Peel the remaining tangerines and slice into rounds, to serve on the side. A spoonful of yoghurt also pairs with it very nicely, if you like.

CLASSIC CAKE

Don't worry if you don't have a bundt tin, a 25cm cake tin lined with greaseproof paper will work just as well.

13

ELEGANT SIMPLICITY

Starter

ORANGE & FENNEL SALAD

With parsley, rocket, ricotta & bresaola

Main

ROASTED FLATFISH

Served with orzo pasta & fragrant olive sauce

Pud

RIPPLED CHEESECAKE

Blackcurrant, booze & a burnt butter biscuit base

Taking the time to thoughtfully bring together beautiful, special, seasonal

ingredients with a confident, delicate touch creates a wonderful harmony.

ORANGE & FENNEL SALAD

PARSLEY, ROCKET, RICOTTA & BRESAOLA

SERVES 8

2 large bulbs of fennel

1 bunch of flat-leaf parsley
(30g)

250g ricotta cheese

20g Parmesan cheese

4 large oranges

1 rustic French baguette
(200g)

70g wild rocket

optional: 16 slices of
bresaola or prosciutto

ON THE DAY Trim and finely slice the fennel, reserving the leafy tops. Place in a large non-stick frying pan on a medium heat with 1 tablespoon of olive oil and a pinch of sea salt and black pepper. Cook for 30 minutes, or until soft, sweet and lightly golden, stirring occasionally, then remove from the heat.

Meanwhile, pop the fennel tops into a bowl of ice-cold water with the parsley leaves. Season the ricotta with black pepper, finely grate over the Parmesan and mash together with a fork. Top and tail the oranges then, standing them on one of the flat ends, trim off the peel. Segment the oranges, squeezing the juice from the inners and peel into the fennel pan. Push the soft fennel to one side and add 2 tablespoons each of red wine vinegar and extra virgin olive oil, scraping up any sticky bits. Cool to room temperature.

TO SERVE Slice and toast the baguette, then spread with the mashed ricotta and divide between plates. Drain the fennel tops and parsley leaves, then gently toss into the pan with the rocket and orange segments, mixing with the soft fennel and the dressing. Pile on to the plates and add the cured meat, if using.

ROASTED FLATFISH

FENNEL, CARROTS & LEMON

The art of cooking a whole fish is simple but incredibly rewarding. The all-round flavour, natural juices and theatre of doing it will make everyone excited. Turbot is the king of flatfish, with a price tag to boot, but I believe everyone should try it at least once in their lifetime. Brill, halibut, sea bass or bream would also be fantastic.

SERVES 8

1 x 2.8–3kg whole turbot, gutted, gills removed

1 tablespoon fennel seeds

4 spring onions

4 baby carrots

2 lemons

50g unsalted butter

ON THE DAY Prep the fish an hour before you want to cook it. Wipe it with kitchen paper, place on a large oiled tray and sprinkle over the fennel seeds, then trim, finely slice and scatter over the spring onions. Use a speed-peeler to slice over the carrots lengthways, then very finely slice and lay over 1 lemon. Drizzle with 2 tablespoons of olive oil, squeeze over the juice of the second lemon and season with sea salt and black pepper. Preheat the oven to 160°C. Cook for 45 to 55 minutes (adjusting the time if your fish is smaller or larger than specified). You'll know it's beautifully cooked when the flesh eases away from the bone. Remove from the oven, dot over the butter, cover, then rest for 20 minutes to be served warm, basting occasionally with the tray liquor.

TO SERVE Use a fork and knife to gently cut and peel back the skin from the top side of the fish. All the milky juices that pour out will add to your natural sauce. Ease random chunks of fish away from the bones, placing them on a large platter and spooning over the spring onions, carrots and lemon. Lift up and remove the spine and bones, then gently spoon out all the fish from the underside. Angle the tray so all the juices are in one corner, season to perfection, tasting and tweaking, then spoon over the platter. Serve with the Orzo pasta (page 234), Fragrant olive sauce (page 237) and a simple salad.

ORZO PASTA

BROAD BEANS, HERBS, SWEET TOMATOES & HARISSA

SERVES 8

1 teaspoon rose harissa

1kg ripe cherry tomatoes,
    on the vine

1 bunch of spring onions

1 bulb of garlic

1 bunch of soft herbs (30g),
    such as basil, dill, mint

500g frozen broad beans
    (or fresh, if it's the season)

500g dried orzo pasta

ON THE DAY Preheat the oven to 150°C. In a large roasting tray, mix the harissa with 1 tablespoon each of red wine vinegar and olive oil and a pinch of sea salt and black pepper. Add the tomatoes on the vines, trim and add the whole spring onions, then break up the garlic, squash the unpeeled cloves and add to the tray. Gently toss together, roast for 1 hour, then remove.

Squeeze the soft garlic flesh out of the skins on to a board, finely chop with the spring onions and most of the herb leaves, then scrape into a large pan. Pour the tomatoes and all the juices from the tray through a coarse sieve into the pan, pushing it all through with the back of a spoon. Keep aside.

TO SERVE Heat up the sauce while you cook the broad beans in a large pan of boiling salted water for 2 minutes. Remove with a slotted spoon, pinching the skin off any larger beans, if you like, while you cook the orzo in the large pan of boiling salted water according to the packet instructions. Drain, pour into the sauce with the beans and turn the heat off, letting the orzo suck up all that flavour. Transfer to a large serving bowl, pick over the remaining herbs and finish with a drizzle of extra virgin olive oil. Serve hot or at room temperature.

FRAGRANT OLIVE SAUCE

CAPERS, GARLIC, CELERY LEAVES & LEMON

— SERVES 10 —

ON THE DAY Drain a <u>180g jar of black stone-in olives</u>, squash and destone, then finely chop about the same size as <u>1 tablespoon of baby capers in brine</u>. Finely grate over the zest of <u>1 lemon</u> and <u>½ a small clove of peeled garlic</u>. Add a few finely chopped <u>soft herb leaves or some inner leaves of celery</u>, then scrape into a bowl, squeeze over the lemon juice, add 2 tablespoons of extra virgin olive oil and a pinch of black pepper and mix well.

RIPPLED CHEESECAKE

BLACKCURRANT, BOOZE & A BURNT BUTTER BISCUIT BASE

SERVES 10–12

100g unsalted butter, plus extra for greasing

200g Hobnobs or Lotus Biscoff biscuits

1 teaspoon vanilla bean paste

170g blackcurrant jam

1 teaspoon golden rum or sloe gin, plus extra to serve

720g light cream cheese

150g Greek-style yoghurt

75g icing sugar

GET AHEAD Grease the base and sides of a 20cm loose-bottomed cheesecake tin with butter. Put the biscuits and vanilla paste into a food processor. Melt the butter in a small non-stick pan on a high heat with 1 teaspoon of finely ground black pepper, letting it bubble away for 2½ minutes, until dark golden. Pour over the biscuits and blitz into crumbs. Tip into the prepared tin, pat and compact across the base with the back of your hand, then let it cool for 5 minutes while you mix 2 teaspoons of jam with the booze (use unsweetened orange juice or a quality cordial instead, for kids), and put aside. Blitz the cream cheese, yoghurt and icing sugar in the processor until just smooth. Spoon two-thirds into the tin, then add the remaining jam to the processor and blitz again. Use a spatula to pile this on top of the cream cheese mixture in the tin, and ripple through with just two swipes, then use the back of the spoon to make peaks and troughs on the surface. Spoon over the boozy jam, rippling through the mixture with a cocktail stick, if you like, then cover and refrigerate overnight.

TO SERVE Release the cheesecake from the tin, slice, and serve. I find it delicious with thimbles of rum or sloe gin to enjoy on the side.

14

HARVEST

FESTIVAL

--------------------------------- *Starter* ---------------------------------

TEAR & SHARE FLATBREAD

With lemon cottage cheese, walnuts, herbs & crunchy veg

--------------------------------- *Main* ---------------------------------

SATISFYING VEGGIE BAKE

--------------------------------- *Pud* ---------------------------------

PRECIOUS PEAR TART

The end of summer gives an abundance of veggies in all shapes and sizes.

Recipes that can embrace a whole rainbow, in a comforting way, are a delight.

TEAR & SHARE FLATBREAD

LEMON COTTAGE CHEESE, HERBS, WALNUTS & CRUNCHY VEG

SERVES 8

600g strong bread flour,
plus extra for dusting

300g cottage cheese

1 lemon

400g crunchy veg, such as
radishes, baby carrots,
baby courgettes, cucumber,
fennel

100g shelled unsalted walnut
halves

1 bunch of soft herbs (30g),
such as dill, chives, fennel
tops, flat-leaf parsley

1 tablespoon nigella seeds

pickled jalapeños, to serve

GET AHEAD Pile the flour into a large bowl with a good pinch of sea salt. Gradually pour in 400ml of warm water, mixing it into the flour with a fork. Knead the dough on a flour-dusted surface for 5 minutes, or until smooth and elastic, then wrap and rest in the fridge overnight (at least 12 hours).

ON THE DAY Spoon the cottage cheese into a serving dish. Finely grate over the lemon zest, squeeze in half the juice and drizzle with 1 tablespoon of extra virgin olive oil. Ripple together and season to perfection, tasting and tweaking. Prep your chosen crunchy veg, trimming and halving or slicing, ready to dunk. Finely grate the walnuts into a small bowl. Pick the herbs into another.

TO SERVE Toast the nigella seeds in a large dry non-stick frying pan on a high heat for 2 minutes, then turn the heat off. Rub a large clean work surface with olive oil, then gently stretch out the dough to the size of a pizza. It should be nice and elastic, so keep picking it up at the edges and stretching and pulling it out, then placing the dough back down, where it should stay in place. You want to create a large thin layer about 40cm x 1 metre – it doesn't have to be perfect. Drizzle the surface with oil, then sprinkle with sea salt, black pepper and the toasted nigella seeds. Pat all over, then, working across from one end to the other, roll the whole thing up into a giant sausage, and twist into a snail shape. Let it relax for 10 minutes, then roll or pat out to 2cm thick. Cook in the frying pan on a medium-low heat for 15 minutes on each side, or until golden and cooked through. Remove to a board, let it cool a little, then use your hands to forcefully smash it in from the sides, meaning you can easily tear it apart. Serve everything at the table and let everyone tear, dip and dunk away.

SATISFYING VEGGIE BAKE

We all need extraordinarily tasty ways to get in the good stuff, and with five of your 5-a-day per portion, this dish makes me very happy.

SERVES 8

3 onions

3 cloves of garlic

3 level teaspoons ground coriander

3 teaspoons olive tapenade

3 mixed-colour peppers

3 sweet potatoes

3 large portobello mushrooms

3 courgettes

3 x 400g tins of plum tomatoes

3 large eggs

500g Greek-style yoghurt

100g feta cheese

1 bunch of oregano (20g)

1 packet of filo pastry (270g)

1 mug of basmati rice (300g)

1 x 400g tin of butter beans

GET AHEAD You can prep this on the day, if you prefer. Peel and finely slice the onions and garlic, and place in a large casserole pan on a medium heat with 1 tablespoon of olive oil, the ground coriander and tapenade, stirring regularly. Alongside, we're going to lightly char our veg in a large dry non-stick pan on a high heat to intensify the flavour, so deseed the peppers, scrub the sweet potatoes, then chop into 3cm chunks with the mushrooms and courgettes. One veg at a time, lightly char all over, moving them into the casserole pan as they're done. Add the tomatoes to the mix, breaking them up with a spoon, along with 2 tin's worth of water. Simmer gently for 30 minutes, or until the sweet potatoes are soft. Season to perfection, tasting and tweaking, leave to cool, then cover. Meanwhile, beat the eggs into the yoghurt, roughly crumble and mix in the feta, then cover. Refrigerate both overnight.

ON THE DAY Assemble the bake as your last prep job. Use half the oregano as a brush to coat the inside of a large roasting tray or baking dish with oil. Layer in all but one of the filo sheets, leaving an overhang and brushing with oil as you go. Evenly sprinkle in the rice, drain and scatter over the beans, then pour in your veggie stew. Scrunch over the remaining sheet of filo and fold in the overhang, brush the top with oil, then cover, until needed.

TO SERVE Preheat the oven to 180°C. Cook the bake on the bottom of the oven for 1 hour. Remove from the oven and use the back of a spoon to crack the top of the pastry, then spoon over the creamy topping. Pick the remaining oregano, rub in a little oil and sprinkle over, then return to the middle of the oven for another 40 minutes, or until golden. Great with a simple salad.

PRECIOUS PEAR TART

ALMOND FRANGIPANE & GINGER NUT CRUST

SERVES 12 WITH LEFTOVER PEARS

200ml elderflower cordial

4cm piece of cinnamon stick

4 fresh bay leaves

4 cloves

1 large orange

12 small ripe pears

240g soft unsalted butter, plus extra for greasing

150g ginger nut biscuits

200g blanched almonds

200g golden caster sugar

2 large eggs

2 teaspoons vanilla bean paste

2 tablespoons plain flour

vanilla ice cream, to serve

GET AHEAD Get yourself a deep pan that will snugly fit all the pears in one layer. Pour in the elderflower cordial and 300ml of water, then add the cinnamon, bay and cloves. Use a speed-peeler to add thick strips of orange peel, then squeeze in the juice. Peel the pears, then trim the bottoms off to give each one a flat base. Sit them in the liquor, cover with a scrunched-up sheet of damp greaseproof paper and simmer gently on a medium heat for 20 minutes, or until soft. Remove the pears from the pan and leave to cool. Gently reduce the syrup until thick, then cool, cover everything and refrigerate overnight.

ON THE DAY Preheat the oven to 180°C. Lightly grease a 25cm loose-bottomed tart tin with butter. Blitz the ginger nuts into a fine crumb in a food processor, pulse in 40g of butter, then tip into the tin, patting it across the base and a little up the sides. Blitz the almonds until super-fine in the processor. Add the remaining butter, along with the sugar, eggs, vanilla paste and flour. Blitz until combined, then spoon evenly into the tin. Cut into six of the pears from the stalk down to the base at 1cm intervals, then fan out, nestling the pears into the frangipane, like in the picture. Spoon a little reserved syrup over each pear, then bake the tart for 50 minutes, or until golden and cooked through (covering the edges with tin foil if they start to get too dark).

TO SERVE Slice and serve warm or cold with the remaining syrup, for drizzling, a scoop of vanilla ice cream, and maybe a little glass of amaretto or vin santo.

LOVE YOUR LEFTOVERS

Save the remaining pears for breakfast, brunch, pud or a cheese plate another day.

15

TABLE FOR TWO

Starter

ELEGANT TUNA CARPACCIO

With miso veg, chilli & lime dressing & sesame

Main

CRISPY DUCK TRAYBAKE

With slow-roasted veg, marmalade & brandy gravy

Pud

CHOCOLATE ORANGE CRÈME BRÛLÉE

Togetherness is about quality, not quantity. Intimate gatherings can be special.

houghtful and surprising. Just don't cook in the nude, it'll end in tears . . .

ELEGANT TUNA CARPACCIO

MISO VEG, CHILLI & LIME DRESSING & SESAME

SERVES 2

1 tablespoon quinoa

1 tablespoon frozen edamame
beans

100g crunchy veg, such as
cucumber, sugar snap peas,
mangetout, carrots

2 level teaspoons white
miso paste

2 teaspoons rice wine vinegar

1 fresh chilli

1cm piece of ginger

1 lime

2 teaspoons sesame oil

2 teaspoons low-salt soy sauce

2 teaspoons sesame seeds

1 x 200g super-fresh chunky
tuna steak

optional: 2 sprigs of shiso,
mint or basil

GET AHEAD You can prep all this on the day, if you prefer. Cook the quinoa in plenty of water according to the packet instructions, adding the edamame for the last 2 minutes, then drain and cool. Take a little time to prep your crunchy veg – it's nice to have a mixture, so use up any veg from the fridge – and finely slice everything as delicately as you can – a speed-peeler can be helpful here. Muddle the miso into the rice vinegar, then scrunch with the prepped veg, quinoa and edamame – the flavours will develop and deepen overnight. To make a dressing, deseed and finely chop the chilli and place in a clean jam jar. Peel and finely grate in the ginger, squeeze in the lime juice, then add the sesame oil and soy and pop the lid on. Toast the sesame seeds in a non-stick frying pan on a high heat until lightly golden, tossing regularly, then remove. Now, sear the tuna for just 20 seconds on each side and edge, turning with tongs, then leave to cool. Cover and refrigerate the veg and tuna overnight.

TO SERVE If you've prepped ahead, get everything out of the fridge 15 minutes before serving. Slice the tuna as finely as you can and arrange around a sharing platter. Pile the dressed veg in the centre, shake up the dressing and spoon over the tuna, then finish with the herb leaves (if using), and toasted sesame seeds.

CRISPY DUCK TRAYBAKE

SLOW-ROASTED VEG, MARMALADE & BRANDY GRAVY

SERVES 2

1 onion

1 large bulb of fennel

4 small carrots, heirloom if
you can get them

2 small Maris Piper potatoes
(100g each)

1 raw beetroot (50g)

2 x 220g duck legs

4 cloves of garlic

½ a bunch of thyme (10g)

1 heaped tablespoon orange
marmalade

1 heaped teaspoon English
mustard

1 tablespoon brandy

1 teaspoon plain flour

300ml chicken stock

1 orange

ON THE DAY Preheat the oven to 170°C. Peel and quarter the onion, trim the fennel and chop into quarters, scrub the carrots, potatoes and beet, halving the beet, quartering the spuds, and leaving the carrots whole. Place in a 25cm x 30cm roasting tray with the duck legs, whole unpeeled garlic cloves and thyme sprigs. Drizzle with 1 tablespoon each of olive oil and red wine vinegar, add a pinch of sea salt and black pepper, and toss to coat. Pull the duck legs to the top, skin side up, cover the tray tightly with tin foil and roast for 1 hour. Remove the foil from the tray, give it all a shake, then cook, uncovered, for 1 more hour, or until the duck is crispy and the veg are cooked through. Turn the oven off, plate up the veg and duck legs, leaving the onions and garlic in the tray and discarding the thyme. Pop the plates in the oven to keep warm.

TO SERVE Squeeze the garlic out of its skins in the tray, then place over a medium heat on the hob. Add the marmalade and mustard, stir until the marmalade has melted, then add the brandy. Carefully flame it, if you wish, then let it cook away. Push the onions to one side, stir in the flour, then gradually add the stock, stirring constantly until smooth. Stir the onions back through, then simmer for 5 minutes, or to the consistency of your liking. Meanwhile, top and tail the orange, then, standing it on one of the flat ends, trim off the peel and segment. Season the gravy to perfection, tasting and tweaking, then add the orange segments and serve right away with the duck and veg.

CHOCOLATE ORANGE CRÈME BRÛLÉE

SILKY, INDULGENT & OH-SO-GOOD

SERVES 2 + 2 LEFTOVER PUDS

100ml double cream

300ml semi-skimmed milk

100g dark chocolate (70%)

4 large eggs

80g golden caster sugar,
plus extra for sprinkling

1 orange

seasonal berries, to serve

GET AHEAD Pour the cream and milk into a non-stick pan, snap in the chocolate, and place on a medium-low heat until the chocolate has melted, whisking regularly. Remove from the heat and allow to cool slightly while you separate the eggs. In a large mixing bowl, whisk the yolks (freeze the whites to make meringues another day) with the sugar and the finely grated orange zest until pale and fluffy. Now, whisking constantly, gradually pour in the chocolate mixture until combined. Return to the pan and place over a low heat, then very gently bring to a simmer, whisking constantly for about 10 minutes, or until you have a custard-like consistency. Divide between four small heatproof cups or two sharing bowls, then cool, cover and leave to set in the fridge overnight.

TO SERVE Sprinkle a little sugar over two of the puds, then melt it under a hot grill or using a blowtorch. Serve with orange segments, berries or cherries. The two extra puds will keep for up to 5 days in the fridge, if you can wait that long!

16

AUTUMNAL FARE

Starter

COMFORTING SQUASH, PORCINI & PEAR SOUP

With chestnut & mushroom croûtes, goat's cheese & crispy sage

Main

SAUSAGE WRAPS

Served with cheesy mash, red slaw & sweet onion gravy

Pud

HOT CHOCOLATE SURPRISE

As the leaves fall, and a chill begins to set in, new produce reveals itself.

Use this opportunity to listen to what your body wants, then joyfully cook it.

COMFORTING SQUASH, PORCINI & PEAR SOUP

CHESTNUT & MUSHROOM CROÛTES, GOAT'S CHEESE & CRISPY SAGE

SERVES 8

Soups are quite out of fashion at dinner parties these days, which is exactly why I think you should rustle up a beautiful homemade version. People have forgotten just how good they can be. This combination is scrumptious in every way – my whole family love it. There are loads of exciting varieties of squash out there so feel free to mix it up, and if you ever get the chance to grow squash, they can be really fun.

1 large butternut squash
(1.5kg)

20g dried porcini mushrooms

½ a cinnamon stick

½ a bunch of sage (10g)

1 onion

2 ripe pears

2 litres chicken or veg stock

4 cloves of garlic

180g vac-packed chestnuts

1 rustic French baguette (200g)

100g crumbly goat's cheese

GET AHEAD You can make this on the day, if you prefer. Carefully halve the squash lengthways and deseed, then peel and chop into 3cm chunks. Place in a colander, toss with a few generous pinches of sea salt (most of the salt will be removed later) and leave for 30 minutes to draw out excess moisture, intensifying the flavour. In a mug, cover the porcini with boiling kettle water.

Put a large deep casserole pan on a medium-high heat with 2 tablespoons of olive oil and the cinnamon stick. Tear in half of the sage leaves, then pat the salty liquor off the squash with kitchen paper, and tip into the sage-infused oil. Cook for 10 minutes, stirring occasionally, while you peel and finely chop the onion, and peel, core and roughly chop the pears. Stir the onion and pear into the pan with 1 tablespoon of oil and cook for another 15 minutes, stirring occasionally. Scoop out, wrap and reserve the porcini, then pour the soaking liquor into the pan, discarding just the last gritty bit. Pour in the stock, bring to the boil, and simmer for a final 30 minutes, discarding the cinnamon stick halfway through. Leave to cool, then cover and refrigerate overnight.

TO SERVE Reheat the soup. Pick the remaining sage leaves into a small non-stick frying pan on a medium heat with 1 tablespoon of oil to crisp up while you peel the garlic and finely chop with the reserved porcini. Remove eight crispy sage leaves for garnish, then add the garlic and porcini to the pan. Once the garlic is lightly golden, crumble in the chestnuts. Add 200ml of water and let it bubble away for 5 minutes, then mash with a fork until you have a pâté-like texture, and season to perfection, tasting and tweaking.

Slice the bread at an angle just over 1cm thick and toast until lightly golden, then divide the chestnut and mushroom mixture on top and crumble over the goat's cheese. Serve with the soup, garnished with the crispy sage leaves.

SAUSAGE WRAPS

Putting a twist on our classic and much-loved bangers and mash, I love the fact that this can be handheld, if you want to make the most of the great outdoors. All the elements are so good together, and the method of grilling the sausages as one, then slicing them up later, means you get a cross-section of gnarly crispy outer and deliciously juicy middle that's to die for.

SERVES 8

2 onions

12 quality meat or veggie sausages, a mixture of types if you can get them

2 teaspoons runny honey

8 wholewheat tortillas

GET AHEAD You can prep this on the day, if you prefer. You need eight skewers – if using wooden ones, soak them in a tray of water first to prevent them burning. Peel the onions, cut into sixths, and break apart into petals. Line up six sausages, interspersing them with half the larger onion petals (keep the smaller, inner bits of onion to chuck into your gravy, page 275, if making). Now, holding them together, carefully push four skewers through all six sausages at regular intervals, meaning you can pick the whole lot up as one. Repeat, then rub with 1 tablespoon of olive oil, cover, and refrigerate overnight.

TO SERVE Cook the sausages on a medium-hot barbecue, under a grill at full whack for 12 minutes, or in the oven at 200°C for 25 to 30 minutes, or until golden and cooked through, turning halfway, and drizzling each set of sausages with 1 teaspoon of honey for the last minute of cooking. Slice between the skewers, giving you eight individual skewers of sausage slices. Briefly warm the tortillas, then spread the mash (page 274) over a wrap, slide the sausages off a skewer on top, add a good handful of slaw (page 274), and wrap the whole thing up. Great served with onion gravy (page 275), for dunking.

ASK YOUR BUTCHER

It's fun to use two or three different types of sausage here – see what your butcher's got and choose whichever ones tickle your fancy.

CHEESY MASH
BUTTER & RED LEICESTER

— SERVES 8 —

ON THE DAY Peel <u>1.5kg of potatoes</u>, chop into even-sized chunks and place in a large pan of salted water, ready to cook.

TO SERVE Bring the water to the boil and cook the potatoes for 15 minutes, or until soft. Drain and leave to steam dry for 2 minutes, then return to the pan and mash well. Add <u>25g of unsalted butter</u> and <u>2 tablespoons of semi-skimmed milk</u>, coarsely grate in <u>120g of red Leicester cheese</u>, mix together, then season to perfection, tasting and tweaking. Once made, you can put the mash in a heatproof bowl, cover with tin foil and place over a pan of gently simmering water to keep warm, until needed.

RED SLAW
CABBAGE, APPLE & PARSLEY

— SERVES 8 —

ON THE DAY Make this just a couple of hours before you want to eat. Very finely slice <u>½ a red cabbage (500g)</u>, then matchstick <u>2 eating apples</u>. Place it all in a bowl, finely chop and add <u>½ a bunch of flat-leaf parsley (15g)</u>, along with <u>1 tablespoon each of wholegrain mustard</u>, extra virgin olive oil and red wine vinegar. Toss and scrunch together to dress the slaw, then season to perfection, tasting and tweaking.

SWEET ONION GRAVY

WORCESTERSHIRE SAUCE & JAM

— SERVES 8 —

GET AHEAD You can make this on the day, if you prefer. Peel and finely slice **3 red onions**, and place in a large non-stick frying pan on a medium heat with 1 tablespoon of olive oil. Cook for 20 minutes, or until soft and sticky, stirring regularly and adding splashes of water or stock, if needed. Add **1 tablespoon of Worcestershire sauce**, stir in **1 heaped tablespoon of plain flour** for 2 minutes, then – stirring constantly – gradually pour in **800ml of veg or beef stock**. Leave it to tick away to the consistency of your liking, then add **1 tablespoon of blackberry or blackcurrant jam** and season to perfection, tasting and tweaking. Cool, cover and refrigerate overnight.

TO SERVE Reheat the gravy in a small pan on a medium-low heat until piping hot, loosening with splashes of water, if needed.

HOT CHOCOLATE SURPRISE

VANILLA ICE CREAM & ORANGE MARMALADE

I love a classic Italian affogato – basically a scoop of ice cream drowned in espresso – but my kids begged me to make them a version with hot chocolate and it was great. Fill your boots, people, this is a good one.

SERVES 8

500g vanilla ice cream

1 litre semi-skimmed milk

3 tablespoons Horlicks powder

3 tablespoons cocoa powder

3 tablespoons soft brown sugar

3 tablespoons orange
  marmalade

GET AHEAD You don't have to do this, but I find it can be helpful to scoop out eight balls of ice cream in advance, then pop them back into the freezer on a tray, so it's already portioned up and ready to go when you come to serve.

TO SERVE Pour the milk into a large pan and bring to a gentle boil over a medium heat, then reduce the heat to low. Whisk in the Horlicks, cocoa powder, sugar and a pinch of sea salt. Let it simmer for 5 minutes, while you place a ball of ice cream in each of eight little cups or bowls. Divide the orange marmalade between them, then pour over the hot chocolate and enjoy.

EMBELLISH IT

Feel free to swap out the marmalade for another preserve of your choice – cherry or apricot jam would work a treat. You can also try adding whisky into the mix for a hot toddy vibe, or a bit of strong espresso as a nod to the traditional affogato.

17

COSY
INDULGENCE

Starter

SALMON TARTARE

Main

MY SUMPTUOUS BEEF BOURGUIGNON

Served with comforting mash & garlicky greens

Pud

SLOE GIN POACHED PLUMS

*With candied puff pastry, toasted almonds
& vanilla ice cream*

Sumptuous textures and comforting flavours dance in the candlelight. This

one's for the grown-ups, so get the red wine flowing, and back off, kids.

SALMON TARTARE

HERB & FENNEL SALAD, EGGS & BAGUETTE

Elegant and light, this is a very tasty starter. I know it can feel daunting to make tartare at home but I promise it's very easy. Give it a go.

SERVES 10

2 large eggs

1 small red onion

2 tablespoons baby capers in brine

2 lemons

2 small bulbs of fennel

1 bunch of soft herbs (30g), such as dill, fennel tops, tarragon, flat-leaf parsley

2 teaspoons Dijon mustard

1 x 800g side of super-fresh salmon, skin off, pin-boned

1–2 rustic French baguettes (200g each)

GET AHEAD You can prep this on the day, if you prefer. Cook the eggs in a pan of boiling salted water for 10 minutes, then cool completely under cold running water, and peel. Peel the onion and finely chop with the capers. Place in a bowl, finely grate over the lemon zest, squeeze over the juice, and stir together. Trim and very finely slice the fennel and place in a bowl of iced water, then pick in the herb leaves – once the ice has melted, drain and wrap the fennel and herbs in a clean tea towel. To make a dressing, in a clean jam jar mix the mustard with 1 tablespoon of red wine vinegar and 3 tablespoons of extra virgin olive oil, then season to perfection, tasting and tweaking, and put the lid on. Slice up the salmon, then chop into ½cm chunks and place in a nice serving bowl. Cover everything and refrigerate overnight.

TO SERVE Slice the baguettes at an angle – serve as is, or toast in the oven. Shake up the dressing, toss with the fennel and herbs, and divide between serving plates with the baguette. Pour the chopped onion and caper mixture into the salmon bowl, add 1 tablespoon of extra virgin olive oil, then mix together well. Season to perfection, tasting and tweaking. Once the salmon is dressed, serve it fairly quickly – in rustic piles, using two spoons to quenelle it, or pressed into a cookie cutter to create a perfect round (see over the page for ideas). Grate over the eggs from a height, to finish.

MY SUMPTUOUS BEEF BOURGUIGNON

BURGUNDY, BACON, BUTTON MUSHROOMS & BABY ONIONS

SERVES 10

1.5kg beef cheeks, trimmed

4 large carrots

4 sticks of celery

4 cloves of garlic

1 onion

2 teaspoons Dijon mustard

4 fresh bay leaves

1 small pinch of ground cloves

750ml Burgundy or Pinot Noir

50g plain flour

20g unsalted butter

6 rashers of smoked
   streaky bacon

200g shallots

400g button mushrooms

½ a bunch of flat-leaf
   parsley (15g)

GET AHEAD Chop the beef cheeks into 5cm chunks. Wash, trim and chop the carrots and celery into 3cm chunks. Peel the garlic and onion, then roughly chop. Place it all in a large bowl with the mustard, bay, cloves, a generous pinch of black pepper and the wine. Mix well, then cover and refrigerate overnight.

ON THE DAY Preheat the oven to 160°C. Pour the contents of the beef bowl into a colander set over another bowl. Pick out just the beef and pat dry with kitchen paper, then toss with the flour. Put a large casserole pan on a medium heat and melt the butter with 2 tablespoons of olive oil. In batches, brown the floured beef all over, turning with tongs and removing to a plate with any crispy bits once browned. Tip the veg into the pan, and cook for 10 minutes, or until starting to caramelize, stirring occasionally and scraping up any sticky bits. Return the beef to the pan, pour over the reserved wine and 750ml of boiling water, then bring to a simmer. Cover with a scrunched-up sheet of damp greaseproof paper and transfer to the oven for around 4 hours, or until the beef is beautifully tender, topping up with splashes of water, if needed.

TO SERVE When the beef is perfect, turn the oven off. Slice the bacon, then place in a large non-stick pan on a medium-high heat. Peel, chop and add the shallots, tossing regularly, then trim and halve or quarter the mushrooms, adding to the pan as you go. Cook for 15 to 20 minutes, or until golden, stirring regularly. Finely chop and toss through the parsley leaves, then pour the contents of the pan over the bourguignon and season to perfection, tasting and tweaking. Serve with the mash (page 290) and Garlicky greens (page 291).

COMFORTING MASH

CELERIAC & POTATO

— SERVES 10 —

ON THE DAY Peel <u>1.5kg of potatoes</u> and <u>1 celeriac (800g)</u>, chop into even-sized chunks and place in a large pan of salted water, ready to cook.

TO SERVE Bring the water to the boil and cook for 15 minutes, or until soft. Drain and leave to steam dry for 2 minutes, then return to the pan and mash well. Stir in <u>25g of unsalted butter</u> and <u>2 tablespoons of semi-skimmed milk</u>, then season to perfection, tasting and tweaking. Once made, you can put the mash in a heatproof bowl, cover with tin foil and place over a pan of gently simmering water to keep warm, until needed.

GARLICKY GREENS

BLANCHED, DRESSED & GRILLED

— SERVES 10 —

GET AHEAD Trim and prep <u>800g of seasonal green veg, such as tenderstem and purple sprouting broccoli, Brussels tops and green beans</u>. Blanch in a large pan of boiling water until almost tender, cooking them separately if using a mixture so you can cook each veg to perfection. Drain well and tip into a large roasting tray. Peel <u>3 cloves of garlic</u> and pound into a paste with a pinch of sea salt in a pestle and mortar. Muddle in 2 tablespoons each of red wine vinegar and olive oil, then pour over the veg and toss well. Cool, cover and store overnight.

TO SERVE Preheat the grill to high. Grill the tray of dressed veg for 5 minutes, or until hot, starting to catch and crisp up, so delicious – keep an eye on them.

SLOE GIN POACHED PLUMS

CANDIED PUFF PASTRY, TOASTED ALMONDS & VANILLA ICE CREAM

SERVES 10

375g ready-rolled puff pastry

1 large egg

175g golden caster sugar

100g flaked almonds

1kg ripe plums

300ml sloe gin

vanilla ice cream, to serve

ON THE DAY Preheat the oven to 180°C. Unroll the pastry on the paper it came in, and cut into ten equal pieces. Use your knife to lightly tap a criss-cross pattern into each piece, then lift the pastry on its paper into a baking tray. Beat the egg and brush all over the pastry, then, from a height, sprinkle over 25g of sugar. Bake for 30 minutes, or until beautifully golden and crisp.

Toast the almonds in a large shallow pan until lightly golden, tossing regularly, then tip into a bowl. Halve and destone the plums, place cut side down in the pan with the remaining 150g of sugar and the sloe gin, then cover and place on a medium heat. Cook for 20 minutes, or until soft, depending on their ripeness.

TO SERVE Spoon the plums on to your plates, then reduce the liquor for a few minutes until syrupy, if needed. Drizzle over the warm plums and serve with the sugared puff and vanilla ice cream, scattered with toasted almonds.

18

CELEBRATION ROAST

SMOKED SALMON OAT BLINIS

With beetroot & celeriac remoulade

EPIC MIXED ROAST

Stuffed chicken, rolled pork belly & topside of beef

VEGGIE CROWN

Slow-roasted veg, Cheddar & chestnuts

*Served with amazing hasselback potatoes & special pigs in blankets,
fennel gratin, beautiful Brussels, delicious carrots & gravy*

BANANA PANETTONE PUDDING

With sticky toffee sauce

When all is said and done, incredible food is merely an excuse to bring loved

ones together and create precious memories. That's really all that matters.

SMOKED SALMON OAT BLINIS

BEETROOT & CELERIAC REMOULADE

SERVES 8

1 tablespoon baby capers
    in brine

2 lemons

250g natural yoghurt

200g celeriac

200g raw beetroot

1 bunch of flat-leaf parsley
    (30g)

1 bunch of dill (20g)

1 mug of porridge oats (150g)

1 mug of self-raising flour
    (250g)

1 large egg

1 mug of semi-skimmed milk
    (400ml)

300g smoked salmon

GET AHEAD You can prep this on the day, if you prefer. Put the capers into a large bowl, squeeze over the juice of 1 lemon and stir in the yoghurt. Peel and coarsely grate the celeriac, then the beets, add to the bowl and mix well, then season to perfection, tasting and tweaking. Finely chop the parsley leaves and most of the dill, and sprinkle on top – but don't toss. Put the oats, flour and a pinch of sea salt into a bowl. Crack in the egg, pour in the milk and whisk into a batter. Cover both and refrigerate overnight.

TO SERVE Put a large non-stick frying pan on a medium heat. In batches, cook tablespoons of the batter in a drizzle of olive oil for 2 minutes on each side, or until puffed up and golden. Cut the remaining lemon into eight wedges, for squeezing over. Mix up the remoulade, stirring through the herbs. Either take it all to the table with the salmon and let people help themselves, or plate up delicate portions, sprinkling over the reserved dill.

EASY SWAPS

Beets and celeriac are a great combo, but feel free to swap in other crunchy numbers like fennel, carrot, white cabbage, or even a little apple or pear.

VEGGIE LOVE

Torn buffalo mozzarella and crushed toasted hazelnuts instead of the salmon will be a joy.

EPIC MIXED ROAST

STUFFED CHICKEN, ROLLED PORK BELLY & TOPSIDE OF BEEF

SERVES 8

3 onions

30g unsalted butter

30g dried cranberries

1 lemon

1 bunch of sage (20g)

30ml cognac

300g panettone or
    breadcrumbs

1 large egg

1.2kg pork belly, deboned,
    skin on and scored

1.5kg whole chicken

1 bunch of thyme (20g)

1.2kg beef topside, deboned,
    fat on, rolled and tied

GET AHEAD For the stuffing, peel and finely slice the onions, then place in a large non-stick pan on a medium heat, season, and dry-fry for 15 minutes, stirring regularly. Add the butter and cranberries, finely grate in the lemon zest and squeeze in the juice, then pick, chop and add the sage leaves. Cook for 5 more minutes, or until the onions are soft. Add the cognac, carefully flame it if you wish, then let it cook away, turn the heat off and leave to cool. Once cool, tear in the panettone, add the egg, and scrunch together well.

Sit the pork belly skin side down on 4 x 60cm lengths of butcher's string. Pat over half the stuffing, then roll up and tie to secure, poking any escaped stuffing back in. Pack the remaining stuffing into the chicken neck cavity, then pull the skin back over it and tuck under the bird. Put the thyme into the other cavity, then tie the legs together with string, also tucking in the wings and tying it around the middle. Cover it all and refrigerate overnight.

ON THE DAY Get all the meat out of the fridge an hour before you start cooking, rubbing each piece with 1 tablespoon of olive oil and seasoning with sea salt and black pepper. Preheat the oven to 190°C. Roast just the pork in a large roasting tray on the middle shelf for 15 minutes, then add the chicken and roast for another 15 minutes. Add the beef, basting the meats with the tray juices, and roast for 1 final hour, or until everything is cooked through and the juices run clear. Remove the meats to a platter, cover with tin foil and a clean tea towel, and rest for 1 hour. You can use the tray to reheat your gravy – skim off excess fat, then simmer the gravy (page 318) on a medium-low heat on the hob until hot through, scraping up the sticky bits. Pour any resting juices into the gravy, then remove the string before carving all the meat.

VEGGIE CROWN

SLOW-ROASTED VEG, CHEDDAR & CHESTNUTS

SERVES 8

*I have to say, I'm pretty proud of this one – it's
a fantastic veggie main inspired by the textures
of a Scottish clootie dumpling, and it also makes
a tasty alternative to stuffing if any meat eaters
fancy a little slice with their meal.*

¼ of a butternut squash (300g)

2 carrots

200g raw beetroot

2 red onions

1 bunch of thyme (20g)

10g dried porcini mushrooms

400g self-raising flour

1 teaspoon baking powder

100g vegetable suet

250g pouch of cooked mixed grains

180g vac-packed chestnuts or shelled unsalted walnut halves

50g Cheddar cheese

1 whole nutmeg, for grating

6 sun-dried tomatoes

1 large egg

150ml semi-skimmed milk

unsalted butter

GET AHEAD Preheat the oven to 180°C. Scrub the squash, carrots and beets, and chop into 3cm chunks. Peel and quarter the onions. Place it all in a roasting tray, keeping each veg separate. Strip over the thyme leaves, drizzle with 2 tablespoons of olive oil, and add a pinch of sea salt and black pepper, jiggling the tray to coat. Roast for 1 hour, then remove and leave to cool.

Soak the porcini in 100ml of boiling kettle water. Place the flour, baking powder, suet and grains in a large bowl, crumble in the chestnuts and add a pinch of salt and pepper. Coarsely grate in the Cheddar and finely grate in half the nutmeg. Scoop out the porcini, finely chop with the sun-dried tomatoes and add to the mix, then pour in the porcini soaking water, discarding just the last gritty bit. Beat the egg into the milk, and stir it all together. Mix in the cool roasted veg, taking care not to break them up, and adding an extra splash of milk to bring it together, if needed. Generously grease a 2-litre non-stick bundt tin, pudding basin or 23cm springform cake tin with butter, pack in the mixture, cover with greaseproof paper and a tight double layer of tin foil, then refrigerate overnight.

TO SERVE Preheat the oven to 190°C. Roast the veggie crown above the meat for 1 hour 15 minutes, or until crisp at the edges, then turn out, slice and serve. It will sit happily, covered, for up to 40 minutes before serving, if needed.

AMAZING HASSELBACK POTATOES

SPECIAL PIGS IN BLANKETS, WALNUT & POLENTA SPRINKLE

SERVES 8 AS A SIDE

2kg Maris Piper potatoes (choose the smallest ones)

4 large sausages (400g total)

optional sausage stuffers: dates, dried cranberries, mustard, chilli, sage, cheese, pickled onions

4 rashers of smoked streaky bacon

optional: small sprigs of rosemary

2 cloves of garlic

1 tablespoon polenta

4 shelled unsalted walnut halves

VEGGIE LOVE

Swap the pigs in blankets for halved veggie sausages. Add for just 20 minutes, grating over melty cheese for the last 5 minutes.

GET AHEAD Preheat the oven to 180°C. Try to choose small potatoes, give them a wash, and if you have any larger ones, cut them in half and use the flat side as a base. To make this process as simple as possible, place a potato on a board between the handles of two wooden spoons, so that when you slice down into the potato the spoons stop the blade from going all the way through. Carefully slice at just under ½cm intervals all the way along. Repeat with all the potatoes, placing them in a large roasting tray as you go. Drizzle with 2 tablespoons of olive oil, season with sea salt and black pepper, and roast for 1 hour, or until the potatoes are golden and tender. Remove and leave to cool.

Twist each sausage in the middle so you can cut each one in half. Now, for a bit of fun, I like to use a small sharp knife to make an incision into each one, creating a little hole ready to stuff with whatever will elevate your sausages to an even higher level of joy. Cut the bacon rashers in half, then, working one at a time, press the side of your knife across each mini rasher to stretch it out. Place a sausage on each, wrap it up, then skewer with a cocktail stick or a sharpened sprig of rosemary. Nestle the wrapped sausages in among the cool potatoes, then cover and refrigerate overnight.

TO SERVE Preheat the oven to 190°C. Peel the garlic and pound up in a pestle and mortar with a small pinch of salt, then mix in the polenta and finely grate in the walnuts. Sprinkle over the potatoes, then drizzle with 1 tablespoon of oil. When the Epic mixed roast (page 302) comes out, roast the potatoes for 1 hour, or until hot and crisp, and the sausages are golden and cooked through.

FENNEL GRATIN

GARLIC, CREAM & CHEESE

SERVES 8 AS A SIDE

2 large bulbs of fennel

1 bulb of garlic

50g cheese (I like a mixture
of Cheddar, Lancashire
and blue)

250ml single cream

GET AHEAD Preheat the oven to 180°C. Trim the fennel bulbs and cut into eighths, reserving any leafy tops in a small bowl of water. Place the fennel in a baking dish with the whole unpeeled garlic cloves, drizzle with 1 tablespoon of olive oil, add a pinch of sea salt and black pepper, toss well with a good splash of water, then arrange in a single layer, cover with tin foil and roast for 1 hour.

Coarsely grate the cheese and mix with the cream. When the fennel comes out, use tongs to squeeze the soft garlic out of the skins, mash it up with a fork and mix through the cream. Let the fennel cool completely, then spoon over the creamy mixture, cover and refrigerate overnight.

TO SERVE Preheat the oven to 190°C. Uncover the fennel and bake for 40 minutes, or until golden, bubbling and hot through. Drain any reserved fennel tops and sprinkle over the dish before serving.

BEAUTIFUL BRUSSELS

CLEMENTINE, NUTMEG & CINNAMON

SERVES 8 AS A SIDE

3 clementines

1 whole nutmeg, for grating

1 cinnamon stick

800g mixed Brussels sprouts
    & tops

GET AHEAD You can do this on the day, if you prefer. Squeeze the clementine juice into a large shallow ovenproof dish. Add 2 tablespoons of extra virgin olive oil, a pinch of sea salt and black pepper and a good grating of nutmeg, then carefully set fire to the cinnamon stick, blow it out, and add to the bowl to infuse. Wash and trim the sprouts, clicking off any tatty outer leaves. Halve the tops, then slice into the stalk of each half for even cooking. Cook the sprouts in a pan of boiling water for 3 minutes, then add the tops leaf side up for another 3 minutes. Drain, refresh under cold running water, then drain again and toss straight into the dressing. Leave to cool, then cover and refrigerate overnight.

TO SERVE Preheat the oven to 190°C. Pop the uncovered dish of Brussels in for 10 minutes, or until hot through. Or, you can remove the cinnamon stick and pop the dish under a hot grill for 20 minutes, and you'll get some tasty crispy edges – your choice. Both ways are delicious.

DELICIOUS CARROTS

MARMALADE, VINEGAR, MUSTARD SEEDS & MELLOW CHILLI

SERVES 8 AS A SIDE

800g carrots

4 fresh red chillies

15g unsalted butter

1 teaspoon mustard seeds

4 fresh bay leaves

1 heaped teaspoon fine-cut
orange marmalade

GET AHEAD You can do this on the day, if you prefer. Wash the carrots and chop into erratic 2cm chunks. Prick the chillies. Place it all in a large non-stick pan on a medium heat with the butter, mustard seeds and bay. Season with sea salt and black pepper, then cook for 15 minutes, or until lightly golden, tossing regularly. Add 100ml of water, put the lid on, and cook for another 15 minutes, or until soft, then turn the heat off, cool, cover and leave overnight.

TO SERVE Uncover the carrots, add the marmalade and 1 tablespoon of red wine vinegar, and reheat over a medium heat on the hob until hot through, about 15 minutes, stirring occasionally and adding a splash of water, if needed.

LOVE YOUR LEFTOVERS

Squash leftover carrots on to hot toasts with ripe avocado and torn mozzarella, or enjoy in a colourful salad. Any leftover chillies will be delicious served with a cheeseboard. Yum.

VEGGIE GRAVY

GET-AHEAD STYLEE

*What's brilliant about this fantastic veggie gravy is you can make it,
reserve what you need for your veggie guests, then reheat the rest in your
tray of roasted meat juices for even more amplified deliciousness.*

SERVES 8 WITH LEFTOVERS

1 leek

1 carrot

1 stick of celery

1 onion

1 veg stock cube

10g dried porcini mushrooms

1 bunch of rosemary (20g)

15g unsalted butter

180g vac-packed chestnuts

½ teaspoon smoked paprika

150ml red wine

2 tablespoons balsamic vinegar

1 tablespoon quince or
  redcurrant jelly

GET AHEAD Trim and wash the leek, carrot and celery, peel the onion, then
roughly chop it all and place in a large non-stick pan on a medium-high heat.
Dry-fry for 15 minutes, or until softened and dark golden, stirring regularly and
adding splashes of water to prevent it sticking, if needed. Meanwhile, crumble
the stock cube into a jug with the porcini and rosemary, then cover with 500ml
of boiling kettle water and leave aside to infuse.

Stir the butter, chestnuts and paprika into the pan. Cook for 5 minutes, then
add the wine, balsamic and jelly. Let the liquid cook away, cool slightly, then
tip the contents of the pan into a blender. Pour in the porcini and the stock,
discarding just the last gritty bit and the rosemary, add 500ml of water and blitz
until very smooth – in batches, if needed. Season to perfection, tasting and
tweaking, then cool, cover and refrigerate for up to 4 days.

TO SERVE Simply reheat the gravy in a pan, or, for bonus flavour, use your tray
of roasting juices from the Epic mixed roast (see page 302 for instructions),
loosening with splashes of water, if needed.

THE FREEZER IS YOUR FRIEND

This gravy freezes really well so get super ahead
or even batch up. Simply defrost and reheat.

BANANA
PANETTONE PUDDING

STICKY TOFFEE SAUCE

SERVES 12

65g soft unsalted butter,
    plus extra for greasing

ground cinnamon

200g golden caster sugar,
    plus extra for sprinkling

3 teaspoons vanilla bean paste

3 large eggs

3 clementines

600ml semi-skimmed milk

optional: smooth whisky,
    brandy, golden rum

4 bananas

150g Medjool dates

500g panettone

15g flaked almonds

150ml single cream

vanilla ice cream, to serve

ON THE DAY In a large mixing bowl, mash 50g of butter with a pinch of cinnamon, 50g of sugar and the vanilla paste. Crack in the eggs, squeeze in the clementine juice, add the milk and whisk together. At this point, you could add a splash of smooth whisky, brandy or golden rum, if you wish. Peel, finely slice and add the bananas, destone, finely chop and add the dates, randomly tear in the panettone, and mix it all together really well. Grease a shallow baking dish (25cm diameter) with a little butter, pour in the mixture, sprinkle over the almonds and a pinch of cinnamon, then cover and refrigerate until needed.

TO SERVE Preheat the oven to 180°C. Bake the pudding for 40 minutes, or until golden and bubbling, then leave to rest for 10 minutes while you make the sauce. Put the remaining 150g of sugar into a small non-stick frying pan with 50ml of water. Place on a medium heat and let the sugar melt until you have a chestnut brown caramel, swirling the pan occasionally – don't be tempted to touch it. Stand back and whisk in the cream until smooth and combined – it will bubble vigorously – then whisk in the remaining 15g of butter. Either pour the sauce over the pudding, or carefully decant it into a cute jug, for pouring at the table. Great with vanilla ice cream, if you so wish.

19

THE WONDER OF COCKTAILS

As I've got older, I've really learnt to appreciate cocktails. The whole industry has grown and become so dynamic. It's really very similar to cooking – yes, it's often precise, but you can have classic cocktails, or you can use nostalgia and humour to mix things up.

First and foremost, and I mean this sincerely, it's always good to test any cocktail you're making for a party. Spend a moment combining wonderful ingredients with care, enjoy the ritual, choose an appropriate glass, and make sure the drink is right for your occasion.

Within this chapter you'll find a really lovely mix of drinks that should enrich any gathering you throw, and act as a nice little icebreaker on arrival. Cheers!

BATCHING UP IS YOUR BEST FRIEND

Some of the world's best cocktail bars batch up their cocktails – let me explain why. It means the day, week or even month before a party or celebration you can combine all the non-perishable ingredients in perfect amounts, so that you're just pouring perfect cocktails over ice and adding a little garnish or topping up to serve, which cuts down on stress and mess. In this chapter, I've noted the recipes that can be batched, if you want to get prepped – simply store in the fridge or freezer (as directed) until needed.

EQUIPMENT

I use a standard cocktail shaker, spoon, sieve, coffee filters, a funnel, jug and clean reusable bottles, which can be cheap as chips, and are widely available. I also think it's important to spoil yourself with a few nice tumblers, coupes and flutes – again super-easy to get hold of these days and they can be very good value. These simple pieces of equipment will allow you to do any of the cocktails within this chapter.

SIMPLE SUGAR SYRUP

Use either demerara or white caster sugar. Mix two parts sugar to one part boiling kettle water in a small pan, then stir over a medium heat until dissolved. Cool, then bottle.

ROYAL MOJITO

— MAKES 1 —

TO ORDER Chill a flute, coupe or coupette by filling with ice. Put <u>50ml of white rum</u>, <u>25ml of freshly squeezed lime juice</u> and <u>15ml of demerara sugar syrup</u> (page 323) in a little jug with the leaves from <u>1 sprig of fresh mint</u> and a couple of ice cubes, then stir to chill the mixture. Remove the ice from your glass, then pour in the drink through a sieve, putting a couple of pretty mint leaves back in. Top up with the <u>fizz of your choice</u> and serve.

BATCH IT The day before, batch up the rum, lime juice and sugar syrup if you want to be able to make multiple drinks at once.

BRAMBLE

— MAKES 1 —

TO ORDER Mix <u>50ml of gin</u>, <u>2 teaspoons of caster sugar syrup</u> (page 323), <u>15ml of freshly squeezed lemon juice</u> and <u>1 teaspoon of blackberry jam or jelly</u> well in a little jug, then pour into a tall glass filled with ice, topping up with <u>soda water</u> before serving. Garnish with <u>1 blackberry</u>, if you like.

COFFEE NEGRONI

— MAKES 6 —

GET AHEAD Mix <u>150ml of gin</u>, <u>150ml of sweet vermouth</u>, <u>150ml of Campari</u> and <u>1 teaspoon of limoncello</u> together. Put a coffee filter (or double layer of kitchen paper) into a funnel, then into a bottle, add <u>50g of fresh coarsely ground coffee</u>, then pour the booze mixture over the coffee and through the filter – this could take up to 1 hour. Keep in the freezer until needed.

TO ORDER Simply pour over ice in a tumbler and, if you wish, you can garnish each cocktail with an <u>orange</u> slice or a strip of peel – use a speed-peeler, gently twisting before adding.

PORNSTAR MARTINI

— MAKES 1 —

TO ORDER Frost a flute by filling it with ice. Mix <u>50ml of vodka</u> with ½ a <u>teaspoon of vanilla bean paste</u>, <u>1 teaspoon of light runny honey</u> and <u>20ml of freshly squeezed lime juice</u>, scoop in the flesh from <u>1 passion fruit</u>, then give it a good shake over ice in a cocktail shaker. Remove the ice from your glass, then strain the drink into it. Top up with <u>Prosecco</u> and serve.

BATCH IT The day before, batch up the vodka, vanilla paste, honey and lime juice if you want to be able to make multiple drinks at once.

FILTHY VODKA MARTINI

— MAKES 6 —

GET AHEAD Mix <u>360ml of vodka</u>, <u>120ml of dry white vermouth</u> and <u>120ml of green olive jar brine</u> together, then bottle and keep in the freezer until needed.

TO ORDER Simple pour into a chilled coupe or coupette (no ice), placing a <u>green olive</u> at the bottom of the glass.

JAMMY MARGARITA

— MAKES 1 —

GET AHEAD Mix <u>50ml of tequila</u>, <u>20ml of Cointreau</u>, <u>35ml of freshly squeezed lime juice</u> and <u>2 teaspoons of strawberry jam</u>, then refrigerate overnight.

TO ORDER Simply pour through a sieve into a tumbler filled with ice.

BATCH IT The day before, batch up the tequila, Cointreau, lime juice and jam if you want to be able to make multiple drinks at once.

CHOCOLATE ORANGE ESPRESSO MARTINI

— MAKES 1 —

GET AHEAD To make cold-brew, mix <u>150g of fresh coarsely ground coffee</u> with <u>300ml of cold water</u>, stir well, then cover and refrigerate overnight.

TO ORDER Filter the cold-brew coffee. Mix together <u>50ml of vodka, rum or amaretto</u>, <u>20ml of coffee liqueur</u> and 50ml of your cold-brew, give it a good shake over ice in a cocktail shaker, then strain into a chilled coupe, coupette or martini glass – you should end up with a nice frothy head. Finish with a fine grating of <u>chocolate orange</u>.

MY MAPLE
OLD FASHIONED

— MAKES 6 —

GET AHEAD Put <u>2 tablespoons of maple syrup</u>, <u>300ml of bourbon</u> and <u>1 teaspoon of angostura bitters</u> into a cocktail shaker and give it a good shake, then bottle, add <u>1 rooibos teabag</u> to infuse, and keep in the freezer until needed.

TO ORDER Remove and discard the teabag, then pour over ice in a tumbler, coupe or martini glass, garnishing each drink with a strip of <u>orange or clementine</u> peel – use a speed-peeler, gently twisting before adding.

FROZEN
MANGO CAIPIRINHA

— MAKES 4 —

TO ORDER Peel and destone <u>1 ripe mango</u>, then place the flesh in a blender with <u>200ml of cachaça</u>, <u>100ml of freshly squeezed lime juice</u>, <u>1 teaspoon of light runny honey</u> and 16 ice cubes (400g total). Blitz until super smooth, then divide between tumblers and serve.

ELEGANT PIÑA COLADA

— MAKES 4 —

GET AHEAD Mix <u>200ml of white rum</u>, <u>40ml of freshly squeezed lime juice</u>, <u>120ml of pineapple juice</u>, <u>120ml of coconut water</u> and <u>30ml of demerara sugar syrup</u> (page 323) together, then pour <u>100ml of almond milk</u> on to the surface of the drink. Put a double layer of kitchen paper into a funnel, then into a bottle, and pour the mixture through it. Keep in the freezer until needed.

ON THE DAY Transfer the bottle from freezer to fridge in the morning to defrost.

TO ORDER Give it a good shake, then simply pour over ice in a tumbler and finish each cocktail with a little grating of <u>nutmeg</u>, if you like.

INGREDIENTS & EQUIPMENT ROUND-UP

THE FREEZER IS YOUR BEST FRIEND

And there are a few basic rules when it comes to really utilizing it well. If you're batch cooking, remember to let food cool thoroughly before freezing, breaking it down into portions so it cools quicker and you can get it into the freezer within 2 hours. Make sure everything is well wrapped, and labelled for future reference. Thaw in the fridge before use, and use within 48 hours. If you've frozen cooked food, don't freeze it again after reheating it.

FRIDGE ORGANIZATION

With some of the meals that have lots of get-ahead elements, you may need to juggle space in the fridge to get everything in. Just remember that uncooked meat and fish should be well wrapped and placed on the bottom shelf to avoid cross-contamination. Any food that is ready to eat, whether it's cooked or it doesn't need to be cooked, should be stored on a higher shelf.

LET'S CHAT EQUIPMENT

You don't need a huge amount of kit to create epic meals. A set of saucepans and non-stick ovenproof frying pans, a griddle and a shallow casserole pan, chopping boards, some sturdy roasting trays and a decent set of knives are the staples. When it comes to making your life easier, a speed-peeler, box grater and pestle and mortar are all fantastic for creating great texture and boosting flavour, and a blender and food processor will always be a bonus, especially if you're short on time! All recipes are tested in fan-assisted ovens. You can find conversions for conventional ovens, °F and gas online.

CELEBRATE QUALITY & SEASONALITY

As is often the case in cooking, using quality ingredients really does make a difference to the success of the recipes. Try to trade up where you can, buying the best meat, fish or veggies you can find. Also, remember that shopping in season always allows your food to be more nutritious, more delicious and more affordable. When it comes to veg and fruit, remember to give everything a nice wash before you start cooking, especially if you're using stuff raw.

MIGHTY MEAT & EGGS

Generally speaking, we should all be striving to eat more plant-based meals that hero veg, beans and pulses. When you're investing in meat, it makes complete sense to me to enjoy the benefits of better-quality organic, free-range or higher-welfare meat. There's no point in eating meat unless the animal was raised well, free to roam, displayed natural behaviours, and lived a healthy life. Some of the cuts in this book require you to go to a butcher, and I cannot recommend this enough – they can be so helpful, they can order stuff in especially for you, and can ensure you have the exact weights you need. When it comes to eggs and anything containing egg, such as noodles and pasta – always choose free-range or organic.

FOCUSING ON FISH

If you eat fish, it's such an incredibly delicious source of protein, but literally the minute it's caught it starts to deteriorate in freshness, so you want to buy it as close to the day of your meal as you can. Make sure you choose responsibly sourced fish wherever possible – look for the MSC logo, or talk to your fishmonger and take their advice. Try to mix up your choices, choosing seasonal, sustainable options as they're available. If you can only find farmed fish, make sure you look for the RSPCA Assured or ASC logo to ensure your fish is responsibly sourced. If eating fish raw, make sure it's super-fresh – I'd recommend telling your fishmonger about the recipe so they can help you.

DIAL UP YOUR DAIRY

With staple dairy products, like milk, yoghurt and butter, please trade up to organic. Unlike meat, it is only slightly more expensive and I couldn't recommend it enough – we're talking about pennies to upgrade. Every time you buy organic, you vote for a better food system that supports the highest standards of animal welfare, where both cows and land are well looked after.

A NOTE FROM JAMIE'S NUTRITION TEAM

Our job is to make sure that Jamie can be super-creative, while also ensuring that all his recipes meet the guidelines we set. Every book has a different brief, and *Together* is all about the joy of good food. These aren't everyday meals – these are for those celebratory occasions when you want to push the boat out for your loved ones. For absolute clarity and so that you can make informed choices, we've presented easy-to-read nutrition info for each dish on the pages that follow.

Food is fun, joyful and creative – it gives us energy and plays a crucial role in keeping our bodies healthy. Remember, a nutritious, balanced diet and regular exercise are the keys to a healthier lifestyle. We don't label foods as 'good' or 'bad' – there's a place for everything – but encourage an understanding of the difference between nutritious foods for everyday consumption and those to be enjoyed occasionally. For more info about our guidelines and how we analyse recipes, please visit jamieoliver.com/nutrition.

Rozzie Batchelar – Senior Nutritionist, RNutr (food)

A BIT ABOUT BALANCE

Balance is key when it comes to eating well. Balance your plate right and keep your portion control in check, and you can be confident that you're giving yourself a great start on the path to good health. It's important to consume a variety of foods to ensure we get the nutrients our bodies need to stay healthy. You don't have to be spot-on every day – just try to get your balance right across the week. If you eat meat and fish, as a general guide for main meals you want at least two portions of fish a week, one of which should be oily. Split the rest of the week's main meals between brilliant plant-based meals, some poultry and a little red meat. An all-vegetarian diet can be perfectly healthy, too.

WHAT'S THE BALANCE

The UK government's Eatwell Guide shows us what a healthy balance of food looks like. Use the figures below as a rough guide to think about the proportion of each food group you consume across the day.

THE FIVE FOOD GROUPS (UK)	PROPORTION*
Vegetables and fruit	39%
Starchy carbohydrates (bread, rice, potatoes, pasta)	37%
Protein (lean meat, fish, eggs, beans, other non-dairy sources)	12%
Dairy foods, milk & dairy alternatives	8%
Unsaturated fats (such as oils)	1%
AND DON'T FORGET TO DRINK PLENTY OF WATER, TOO	

* Please note: the remaining 3% is made up of food to be enjoyed occasionally.

VEGETABLES & FRUIT

To live a good, healthy life, vegetables and fruit should sit right at the heart of your diet. Veg and fruit come in all kinds of colours, shapes, sizes, flavours and textures, and contain different vitamins and minerals, which each play a part in keeping our bodies healthy and optimal, so variety is key. Eat the rainbow, mixing up your choices as much as you can and embracing the seasons so you're getting produce at its best and its most nutritious. As an absolute minimum, aim for at least 5 portions of fresh, frozen or tinned veg and fruit every day of the week, enjoying more wherever possible. 80g (or a large handful) counts as one portion. You can also count one 30g portion of dried fruit, one 80g portion of beans or pulses, and 150ml of unsweetened veg or fruit juice per day.

STARCHY CARBOHYDRATES

Carbs provide us with a large proportion of the energy needed to make our bodies move, and to ensure our organs have the fuel they need to function. When you can, choose fibre-rich wholegrain and wholewheat varieties. 260g is the recommended daily amount of carbohydrates for the average adult, with up to 90g coming from total sugars, which includes natural sugars found in whole fruit, milk and milk products, and no more than 30g of free sugars. Free sugars are those added to food and drink, including sugar found in honey, syrups, fruit juice and smoothies. Fibre is classified as a carbohydrate and is mainly found in plant-based foods such as wholegrain carbohydrates, veg and fruit. It helps to keep our digestive systems healthy, control our blood-sugar levels and maintain healthy cholesterol levels. Adults should be aiming for at least 30g each day.

PROTEIN

Think of protein as the building blocks of our bodies – it's used for everything that's important to how we grow and repair. Try to vary your proteins and include vegetarian sources. With animal-based proteins, choose lean cuts where you can, limit processed meat and aim to eat at least two portions of fish each week, one of which should be oily. The requirement for an average woman aged 19 to 50 is 45g per day, with 55g for men in the same age bracket.

DAIRY FOODS, MILK & DAIRY ALTERNATIVES

This food group offers an amazing array of nutrients when eaten in the right amounts. Favour organic milk and yoghurt, and small amounts of cheese in this category; the lower-fat varieties (with no added sugar) are equally brilliant and worth embracing. If opting for plant-based versions, I think it's great that we have choice, but please don't be under the illusion that nutritionally you're swapping one milk for another. To bridge the gap to what is essentially flavoured water, please look for a fortified, unsweetened option.

UNSATURATED FATS

While we only need small amounts, we do require healthier fats. Choose unsaturated sources where you can, such as olive and liquid vegetable oils, nuts, seeds, avocado and omega-3 rich oily fish. Generally speaking, it's recommended that the average woman has no more than 70g of fat per day, with less than 20g of that from saturated fat, and the average man no more than 90g, with less than 30g from saturates.

DRINK PLENTY OF WATER

To be the best you can be, stay hydrated. Water is essential to life, and to every function of the human body! In general, women aged 14 and over need at least 2 litres per day and men in the same age bracket need at least 2.5 litres per day.

ENERGY & NUTRITION INFO

The average woman needs 2,000 calories a day, while the average man needs roughly 2,500. These figures are a rough guide, and what we eat needs to be considered in relation to factors like age, build, lifestyle and activity levels.

NUTRITION

HONEY FOCACCIA

ENERGY	FAT	SAT FAT	PROTEIN	CARBS	SUGARS	SALT	FIBRE
192kcal	4g	0.7g	5.2g	35.9g	5.1g	0.3g	1.3g

JERKED ROAST PORK

ENERGY	FAT	SAT FAT	PROTEIN	CARBS	SUGARS	SALT	FIBRE
333kcal	20.8g	7.2g	21.4g	16.4g	10.2g	0.3g	2.6g

EASY BAKED EGGS

ENERGY	FAT	SAT FAT	PROTEIN	CARBS	SUGARS	SALT	FIBRE
181kcal	15.2g	3.4g	8.7g	3.3g	2.9g	0.6g	0.9g

SUBLIME KALE SALAD

ENERGY	FAT	SAT FAT	PROTEIN	CARBS	SUGARS	SALT	FIBRE
208kcal	11.4g	3.3g	9.9g	18.6g	1.6g	0.8g	1.7g

PERFECT PEPPER PICKLE

ENERGY	FAT	SAT FAT	PROTEIN	CARBS	SUGARS	SALT	FIBRE
11kcal	0.1g	0g	0.3g	2g	1.8g	0.5g	0.6g

PILLOWY MERINGUES

ENERGY	FAT	SAT FAT	PROTEIN	CARBS	SUGARS	SALT	FIBRE
268kcal	11.3g	3.6g	5.9g	38.7g	38g	0.3g	0.5g

PEACH TEA JUG

ENERGY	FAT	SAT FAT	PROTEIN	CARBS	SUGARS	SALT	FIBRE
136kcal	0g	0g	0.9g	15.3g	15.1g	0.1g	0g

WONDERFUL WARM SALAD

ENERGY	FAT	SAT FAT	PROTEIN	CARBS	SUGARS	SALT	FIBRE
318kcal	14.9g	4.4g	9.5g	38.1g	17.4g	1.2g	3.8g

CHICKEN, SAUSAGE & BACON PUFF PIE

ENERGY	FAT	SAT FAT	PROTEIN	CARBS	SUGARS	SALT	FIBRE
699kcal	35.2g	14g	35.6g	60.4g	9.2g	1.8g	4.2g

SPRING VEG

ENERGY	FAT	SAT FAT	PROTEIN	CARBS	SUGARS	SALT	FIBRE
213kcal	5.5g	1.2g	10.8g	32.1g	5.4g	0.1g	6.8g

VEG À LA GRECQUE

ENERGY	FAT	SAT FAT	PROTEIN	CARBS	SUGARS	SALT	FIBRE
81kcal	2.2g	0.4g	3.8g	12.8g	7.6g	0.4g	5.3g

RHUBARB & CUSTARD FLOATING ISLANDS

ENERGY	FAT	SAT FAT	PROTEIN	CARBS	SUGARS	SALT	FIBRE
304kcal	7.2g	1.8g	6.8g	54.9g	47.8g	0.5g	1.5g

FRAGRANT SQUASH CURRY

ENERGY	FAT	SAT FAT	PROTEIN	CARBS	SUGARS	SALT	FIBRE
159kcal	6g	3g	5g	22.6g	11.4g	0.3g	5.2g

GOLDEN PANEER

ENERGY	FAT	SAT FAT	PROTEIN	CARBS	SUGARS	SALT	FIBRE
168kcal	11.4g	5.9g	10.8g	6g	4.9g	0.3g	0.6g

SMOKY AUBERGINE DAAL

ENERGY	FAT	SAT FAT	PROTEIN	CARBS	SUGARS	SALT	FIBRE
132kcal	2.8g	0.4g	9.2g	17.6g	2.8g	0g	5.8g

FLUFFY COCONUT RICE

ENERGY	FAT	SAT FAT	PROTEIN	CARBS	SUGARS	SALT	FIBRE
311kcal	4.7g	3.2g	7.3g	64.4g	1.7g	0.4g	0.8g

FENNEL NAAN

ENERGY	FAT	SAT FAT	PROTEIN	CARBS	SUGARS	SALT	FIBRE
320kcal	4.6g	2.1g	10.2g	64.1g	2.4g	0.7g	2.6g

CHOPPED SALAD

ENERGY	FAT	SAT FAT	PROTEIN	CARBS	SUGARS	SALT	FIBRE
34kcal	1.2g	0.2g	1.7g	4.4g	2.7g	0.1g	1.2g

CARROT RAITA

ENERGY	FAT	SAT FAT	PROTEIN	CARBS	SUGARS	SALT	FIBRE
47kcal	2.6g	1.2g	2.2g	4.3g	3.5g	0.1g	0.5g

MANGO CHUTNEY
Page **59**

ENERGY	FAT	SAT FAT	PROTEIN	CARBS	SUGARS	SALT	FIBRE
30kcal	0.1g	0g	0.2g	7.4g	6.7g	0.3g	0.3g

SPICED DUST (per tablespoon)
Page **78**

ENERGY	FAT	SAT FAT	PROTEIN	CARBS	SUGARS	SALT	FIBRE
13kcal	0.6g	0.3g	0.6g	1.7g	1.4g	0g	0.4g

MINTED MANGO FRO-YO
Page **61**

ENERGY	FAT	SAT FAT	PROTEIN	CARBS	SUGARS	SALT	FIBRE
132kcal	6.5g	1.8g	3g	16.3g	15.8g	0.1g	0.5g

TEQUILA MICHELADA
Page **79**

ENERGY	FAT	SAT FAT	PROTEIN	CARBS	SUGARS	SALT	FIBRE
87kcal	0.1g	0g	0.4g	1.7g	1.6g	0.1g	0.5g

SLOW-COOKED PORK BELLY
Page **66**

ENERGY	FAT	SAT FAT	PROTEIN	CARBS	SUGARS	SALT	FIBRE
327kcal	25.8g	9.2g	24g	0.2g	0g	0.6g	0.4g

CHEESE PUFFS
Page **84**

ENERGY	FAT	SAT FAT	PROTEIN	CARBS	SUGARS	SALT	FIBRE
220kcal	14g	7.9g	10g	14.8g	0.4g	0.7g	0.6g

BLACK BEANS & CHEESE
Page **72**

ENERGY	FAT	SAT FAT	PROTEIN	CARBS	SUGARS	SALT	FIBRE
62kcal	1.7g	1g	4g	3.4g	0.4g	0.2g	4.1g

TENDER ASPARAGUS
Page **86**

ENERGY	FAT	SAT FAT	PROTEIN	CARBS	SUGARS	SALT	FIBRE
282kcal	18.9g	3.7g	14.1g	14.1g	3.1g	0.8g	0.2g

HOMEMADE TORTILLAS
Page **73**

ENERGY	FAT	SAT FAT	PROTEIN	CARBS	SUGARS	SALT	FIBRE
152kcal	1.6g	0.2g	3.8g	31.7g	0.6g	0.2g	2.5g

STUFFED SALMON
Page **90**

ENERGY	FAT	SAT FAT	PROTEIN	CARBS	SUGARS	SALT	FIBRE
313kcal	20.6g	3.5g	31.4g	0.1g	0.1g	1g	0.1g

ROASTED PINEAPPLE
Page **74**

ENERGY	FAT	SAT FAT	PROTEIN	CARBS	SUGARS	SALT	FIBRE
62kcal	1.4g	0.2g	1.6g	11.6g	10g	0.2g	2.4g

POTATO SALAD
Page **92**

ENERGY	FAT	SAT FAT	PROTEIN	CARBS	SUGARS	SALT	FIBRE
180kcal	4.3g	0.9g	4.1g	33.2g	3.6g	0.4g	2g

GREEN SALSA
Page **75**

ENERGY	FAT	SAT FAT	PROTEIN	CARBS	SUGARS	SALT	FIBRE
25kcal	2.2g	0.3g	0.3g	0.9g	0.9g	0g	0.2g

ROASTED TOMATOES
Page **92**

ENERGY	FAT	SAT FAT	PROTEIN	CARBS	SUGARS	SALT	FIBRE
42kcal	1.8g	0.2g	1.2g	5.6g	4.6g	0.3g	1.6g

RED CABBAGE
Page **75**

ENERGY	FAT	SAT FAT	PROTEIN	CARBS	SUGARS	SALT	FIBRE
16kcal	1.2g	0.2g	0.3g	1.2g	1.1g	0g	0.6g

TASTY GREENS
Page **93**

ENERGY	FAT	SAT FAT	PROTEIN	CARBS	SUGARS	SALT	FIBRE
112kcal	8.7g	1.2g	3g	7.1g	2.1g	0.1g	3g

CHOCOLATE SEMIFREDDO
Page **76**

ENERGY	FAT	SAT FAT	PROTEIN	CARBS	SUGARS	SALT	FIBRE
211kcal	13.4g	7.6g	4.2g	19.8g	17.1g	0.1g	0.3g

WIMBLEDON SUMMER PUDDING
Page **94**

ENERGY	FAT	SAT FAT	PROTEIN	CARBS	SUGARS	SALT	FIBRE
236kcal	1.4g	0.2g	3.7g	50.7g	35.6g	0.3g	4.2g

HAZELNUT BRITTLE (per tablespoon)
Page **78**

ENERGY	FAT	SAT FAT	PROTEIN	CARBS	SUGARS	SALT	FIBRE
77kcal	3.4g	0.3g	0.8g	11.6g	11.5g	0g	0.4g

PECORINO
Page **102**

ENERGY	FAT	SAT FAT	PROTEIN	CARBS	SUGARS	SALT	FIBRE
85kcal	5.1g	3.2g	3.3g	6.4g	6.3g	0.7g	0.2g

FIGS & HONEY

ENERGY	FAT	SAT FAT	PROTEIN	CARBS	SUGARS	SALT	FIBRE
51kcal	2.9g	0.6g	3g	3.7g	3.7g	0.5g	0.5g

DRESSED OLIVES

ENERGY	FAT	SAT FAT	PROTEIN	CARBS	SUGARS	SALT	FIBRE
39kcal	4.2g	0.6g	0.2g	0g	0g	0.6g	0g

BABY MOZZARELLA

ENERGY	FAT	SAT FAT	PROTEIN	CARBS	SUGARS	SALT	FIBRE
136kcal	12.2g	4.4g	5.9g	0.6g	0.4g	0.6g	0.6g

BORLOTTI BEANS

ENERGY	FAT	SAT FAT	PROTEIN	CARBS	SUGARS	SALT	FIBRE
73kcal	3.7g	0.5g	4g	6g	0.6g	0g	3.4g

GRIDDLED PEPPERS

ENERGY	FAT	SAT FAT	PROTEIN	CARBS	SUGARS	SALT	FIBRE
33kcal	2.1g	0.3g	0.5g	2.6g	2.3g	0g	0.6g

DRESSED CHICKPEAS

ENERGY	FAT	SAT FAT	PROTEIN	CARBS	SUGARS	SALT	FIBRE
118kcal	6g	0.9g	4.8g	11.3g	0.5g	0g	3.4g

CREAMY BEAN DIP

ENERGY	FAT	SAT FAT	PROTEIN	CARBS	SUGARS	SALT	FIBRE
97kcal	4.3g	0.7g	4.7g	9.8g	0.5g	0g	3.3g

ROSEMARY TOASTS

ENERGY	FAT	SAT FAT	PROTEIN	CARBS	SUGARS	SALT	FIBRE
101kcal	1.6g	0.2g	3.5g	17.4g	0.8g	0.3g	0g

BALSAMIC ONIONS

ENERGY	FAT	SAT FAT	PROTEIN	CARBS	SUGARS	SALT	FIBRE
37kcal	2.2g	0.3g	0.4g	3.7g	3.1g	0.4g	0.6g

DRESSED ARTICHOKES

ENERGY	FAT	SAT FAT	PROTEIN	CARBS	SUGARS	SALT	FIBRE
24kcal	1.7g	0.2g	0.6g	0.8g	0.1g	0.7g	1.4g

EFFORTLESSY ELEGANT PASTA

ENERGY	FAT	SAT FAT	PROTEIN	CARBS	SUGARS	SALT	FIBRE
410kcal	25.4g	10.9g	11.1g	33.5g	1.1g	0.3g	2.1g

PANETTONE FRENCH TOAST

ENERGY	FAT	SAT FAT	PROTEIN	CARBS	SUGARS	SALT	FIBRE
290kcal	15.1g	8g	8g	31.6g	22.7g	0.4g	0.6g

BLOODY MARY CRUMPETS

ENERGY	FAT	SAT FAT	PROTEIN	CARBS	SUGARS	SALT	FIBRE
311kcal	13.1g	4.8g	24.7g	25.4g	5.8g	2.9g	0.3g

ROASTED RUMP STEAK

ENERGY	FAT	SAT FAT	PROTEIN	CARBS	SUGARS	SALT	FIBRE
347kcal	25.2g	11.2g	29.5g	0.7g	0.5g	0.4g	0g

GRILLED & ROASTED POTATOES

ENERGY	FAT	SAT FAT	PROTEIN	CARBS	SUGARS	SALT	FIBRE
239kcal	5g	0.8g	5.8g	45.2g	1.8g	0.4g	3.2g

ROASTED RED ONIONS

ENERGY	FAT	SAT FAT	PROTEIN	CARBS	SUGARS	SALT	FIBRE
94kcal	3.8g	1.2g	1.6g	14.2g	11.2g	0.3g	3g

WATERCRESS SAUCE

ENERGY	FAT	SAT FAT	PROTEIN	CARBS	SUGARS	SALT	FIBRE
114kcal	7.1g	1.1g	3.2g	9.1g	1.5g	1.3g	0.8g

AMAZING ROUND LETTUCE SALAD

ENERGY	FAT	SAT FAT	PROTEIN	CARBS	SUGARS	SALT	FIBRE
79kcal	4.4g	2.7g	6.5g	3.3g	3.3g	0.7g	1.9g

CARAMELIZED PINEAPPLE TARTLETS

ENERGY	FAT	SAT FAT	PROTEIN	CARBS	SUGARS	SALT	FIBRE
167kcal	5.3g	1.9g	3.6g	28.5g	16.8g	0.2g	0.7g

SCRUMPTIOUS GARLIC BREAD

ENERGY	FAT	SAT FAT	PROTEIN	CARBS	SUGARS	SALT	FIBRE
191kcal	3.6g	1.5g	6.9g	34.5g	1.8g	0.4g	1.8g

CRISPY PESTO CHICKEN

ENERGY	FAT	SAT FAT	PROTEIN	CARBS	SUGARS	SALT	FIBRE
457kcal	16.9g	3.3g	44.8g	32.1g	2.1g	1g	1.5g

COMFORTING RED RICE

ENERGY	FAT	SAT FAT	PROTEIN	CARBS	SUGARS	SALT	FIBRE
368kcal	8.5g	4g	13.5g	62g	12.5g	0.3g	7.7g

BUDDY'S GREEN SALAD

ENERGY	FAT	SAT FAT	PROTEIN	CARBS	SUGARS	SALT	FIBRE
43kcal	2g	0.3g	1.3g	5.6g	4.1g	0.1g	1.3g

ESSEX ETON MESS

ENERGY	FAT	SAT FAT	PROTEIN	CARBS	SUGARS	SALT	FIBRE
385kcal	17.8g	10.8g	14.4g	42.5g	40.2g	0.2g	4.7g

RAINBOW TOMATO CROSTINI

ENERGY	FAT	SAT FAT	PROTEIN	CARBS	SUGARS	SALT	FIBRE
154kcal	5.2g	3.2g	7.3g	19.1g	2.3g	0.7g	1.2g

SLOW-ROASTED LAMB

ENERGY	FAT	SAT FAT	PROTEIN	CARBS	SUGARS	SALT	FIBRE
458kcal	28.5g	12.5g	30g	17.4g	1.3g	0.7g	1g

LEMON POTATOES

ENERGY	FAT	SAT FAT	PROTEIN	CARBS	SUGARS	SALT	FIBRE
176kcal	2.6g	0.4g	4.2g	36g	1.2g	0.2g	2.8g

DRESSED BEANS

ENERGY	FAT	SAT FAT	PROTEIN	CARBS	SUGARS	SALT	FIBRE
44kcal	2.5g	0.4g	2.1g	3.2g	2.2g	0.2g	3.4g

APRICOT SAUCE

ENERGY	FAT	SAT FAT	PROTEIN	CARBS	SUGARS	SALT	FIBRE
40kcal	2.3g	0.3g	0.5g	4.7g	4.6g	0.2g	0.9g

GREEN SAUCE

ENERGY	FAT	SAT FAT	PROTEIN	CARBS	SUGARS	SALT	FIBRE
64kcal	6.5g	0.9g	0.8g	0.5g	0.3g	0.3g	0.2g

YOGHURT PANNA COTTA

ENERGY	FAT	SAT FAT	PROTEIN	CARBS	SUGARS	SALT	FIBRE
155kcal	8.2g	5.3g	4.7g	16.4g	16.4g	0.1g	1.3g

WATERMELON SKEWERS

ENERGY	FAT	SAT FAT	PROTEIN	CARBS	SUGARS	SALT	FIBRE
83kcal	4.4g	2.8g	4.1g	7.8g	6.5g	0.7g	0.7g

DUKKAH ROAST CHICKEN

ENERGY	FAT	SAT FAT	PROTEIN	CARBS	SUGARS	SALT	FIBRE
248kcal	8.5g	1.7g	38.2g	5g	4.5g	1g	1.1g

ROASTED SQUASH

ENERGY	FAT	SAT FAT	PROTEIN	CARBS	SUGARS	SALT	FIBRE
94kcal	2.4g	0.4g	2.4g	17g	9.2g	0.4g	3.2g

SMASHED AUBERGINE

ENERGY	FAT	SAT FAT	PROTEIN	CARBS	SUGARS	SALT	FIBRE
78kcal	5.7g	0.9g	2.8g	4.3g	2.8g	0.1g	3g

AMAZING DUKKAH

ENERGY	FAT	SAT FAT	PROTEIN	CARBS	SUGARS	SALT	FIBRE
83kcal	8g	0.9g	2.6g	0.7g	0.5g	0.7g	0.7g

CRISPY CHICKPEA RICE

ENERGY	FAT	SAT FAT	PROTEIN	CARBS	SUGARS	SALT	FIBRE
239kcal	3.4g	0.5g	6.8g	48.1g	0.3g	0.3g	2.5g

APPLE & BRAMBLE CRUMBLE TART

ENERGY	FAT	SAT FAT	PROTEIN	CARBS	SUGARS	SALT	FIBRE
365kcal	15.8g	9g	5g	55g	28.2g	0.1g	3.4g

EXTRAORDINARY SEAFOOD PARCELS

ENERGY	FAT	SAT FAT	PROTEIN	CARBS	SUGARS	SALT	FIBRE
289kcal	13.5g	6.5g	33.8g	7.9g	4.6g	1.7g	1.4g

TENDER STICKY AUBERGINES

ENERGY	FAT	SAT FAT	PROTEIN	CARBS	SUGARS	SALT	FIBRE
98kcal	3.4g	0.6g	2.7g	16.7g	9.7g	0.2g	7g

NOODLE RICE CAKE
Page **200**

ENERGY	FAT	SAT FAT	PROTEIN	CARBS	SUGARS	SALT	FIBRE
318kcal	6g	1g	7.6g	63.2g	0.2g	0.6g	0.7g

RAINBOW SLAW
Page **201**

ENERGY	FAT	SAT FAT	PROTEIN	CARBS	SUGARS	SALT	FIBRE
123kcal	5.4g	1.3g	4g	15.6g	12.8g	0.4g	3g

SILKY WHITE CHOCOLATE MOUSSE
Page **202**

ENERGY	FAT	SAT FAT	PROTEIN	CARBS	SUGARS	SALT	FIBRE
318kcal	17g	7.6g	14g	28.9g	28.3g	0.1g	0g

QUICHE
Page **208**

ENERGY	FAT	SAT FAT	PROTEIN	CARBS	SUGARS	SALT	FIBRE
285kcal	17.7g	9.8g	9.8g	23.5g	4.5g	0.5g	2g

JAM JAR PRAWN COCKTAILS
Page **212**

ENERGY	FAT	SAT FAT	PROTEIN	CARBS	SUGARS	SALT	FIBRE
237kcal	13.2g	2.2g	14.8g	15.3g	6.8g	2.3g	2g

GREENHOUSE COUSCOUS SALAD
Page **216**

ENERGY	FAT	SAT FAT	PROTEIN	CARBS	SUGARS	SALT	FIBRE
207kcal	7.7g	3.3g	8g	28.4g	4.6g	1.1g	2.3g

PRETTY PICKLED VEG
Page **218**

ENERGY	FAT	SAT FAT	PROTEIN	CARBS	SUGARS	SALT	FIBRE
86kcal	0.2g	0g	0.8g	3.1g	2g	0.1g	0.7g

SAVOURY SEEDED CRACKERS
Page **220**

ENERGY	FAT	SAT FAT	PROTEIN	CARBS	SUGARS	SALT	FIBRE
133kcal	5.2g	0.7g	3.1g	19.5g	0.4g	0.4g	1.1g

TANGERINE DREAM CAKE
Page **222**

ENERGY	FAT	SAT FAT	PROTEIN	CARBS	SUGARS	SALT	FIBRE
348kcal	22.3g	9.3g	6.9g	32.1g	20.1g	0.4g	0.6g

ORANGE & FENNEL SALAD
Page **228**

ENERGY	FAT	SAT FAT	PROTEIN	CARBS	SUGARS	SALT	FIBRE
234kcal	11.3g	3.7g	8.5g	25.4g	6.4g	0.7g	4.3g

ROASTED FLATFISH
Page **232**

ENERGY	FAT	SAT FAT	PROTEIN	CARBS	SUGARS	SALT	FIBRE
287kcal	14.4g	5.3g	37.8g	2.8g	1.5g	0.4g	0.8g

ORZO PASTA
Page **234**

ENERGY	FAT	SAT FAT	PROTEIN	CARBS	SUGARS	SALT	FIBRE
308kcal	5.7g	0.8g	12.9g	53.7g	5.4g	0.4g	7.3g

FRAGRANT OLIVE SAUCE
Page **237**

ENERGY	FAT	SAT FAT	PROTEIN	CARBS	SUGARS	SALT	FIBRE
33kcal	3.6g	0.5g	0.2g	0.1g	0g	0.4g	0.1g

RIPPLED CHEESECAKE
Page **238**

ENERGY	FAT	SAT FAT	PROTEIN	CARBS	SUGARS	SALT	FIBRE
304kcal	17.6g	9.5g	6.9g	29g	22.9g	0.7g	1.5g

TEAR & SHARE FLATBREAD
Page **244**

ENERGY	FAT	SAT FAT	PROTEIN	CARBS	SUGARS	SALT	FIBRE
407kcal	13.1g	2.3g	16g	60.6g	4g	0.6g	3.1g

SATISFYING VEGGIE BAKE
Page **246**

ENERGY	FAT	SAT FAT	PROTEIN	CARBS	SUGARS	SALT	FIBRE
580kcal	13.7g	5.3g	24g	96.2g	21.3g	1.3g	11.2g

PRECIOUS PEAR TART
Page **250**

ENERGY	FAT	SAT FAT	PROTEIN	CARBS	SUGARS	SALT	FIBRE
444kcal	29g	12.3g	6g	42.7g	34g	0.2g	1.8g

ELEGANT TUNA CARPACCIO
Page **256**

ENERGY	FAT	SAT FAT	PROTEIN	CARBS	SUGARS	SALT	FIBRE
253kcal	12.7g	2.5g	17.7g	7.6g	2.6g	1.2g	1.8g

CRISPY DUCK TRAYBAKE
Page **260**

ENERGY	FAT	SAT FAT	PROTEIN	CARBS	SUGARS	SALT	FIBRE
698kcal	19.4g	5.2g	49g	86.6g	30.2g	2.5g	18.6g

CHOCOLATE ORANGE CRÈME BRÛLÉE
Page **262**

ENERGY	FAT	SAT FAT	PROTEIN	CARBS	SUGARS	SALT	FIBRE
414kcal	27.1g	13.7g	8.9g	39.8g	39.6g	0.2g	1g

COMFORTING SQUASH, PORCINI & PEAR SOUP

Page 268

ENERGY	FAT	SAT FAT	PROTEIN	CARBS	SUGARS	SALT	FIBRE
325kcal	10.1g	3.4g	15.3g	44.8g	16.7g	1g	5.6g

SAUSAGE WRAPS

Page 272

ENERGY	FAT	SAT FAT	PROTEIN	CARBS	SUGARS	SALT	FIBRE
422kcal	19.4g	6.6g	18.8g	41.4g	7.9g	1.8g	5.2g

CHEESY MASH

Page 274

ENERGY	FAT	SAT FAT	PROTEIN	CARBS	SUGARS	SALT	FIBRE
230kcal	8.5g	5.1g	7.6g	32.6g	1.3g	0.3g	2.4g

RED SLAW

Page 274

ENERGY	FAT	SAT FAT	PROTEIN	CARBS	SUGARS	SALT	FIBRE
46kcal	2.1g	0.3g	1.1g	5.9g	5.7g	0.1g	2.2g

SWEET ONION GRAVY

Page 275

ENERGY	FAT	SAT FAT	PROTEIN	CARBS	SUGARS	SALT	FIBRE
69kcal	2g	0.3g	1.9g	11.4g	6.1g	0.7g	1.1g

HOT CHOCOLATE SURPRISE

Page 278

ENERGY	FAT	SAT FAT	PROTEIN	CARBS	SUGARS	SALT	FIBRE
232kcal	7.8g	4.8g	7.3g	35.9g	33.2g	0.6g	0.4g

SALMON TARTARE

Page 284

ENERGY	FAT	SAT FAT	PROTEIN	CARBS	SUGARS	SALT	FIBRE
273kcal	15.3g	2.6g	20.7g	13g	2.6g	0.5g	2.4g

MY SUMPTUOUS BEEF BOURGUIGNON

Page 288

ENERGY	FAT	SAT FAT	PROTEIN	CARBS	SUGARS	SALT	FIBRE
345kcal	13.2g	4.8g	34.4g	11g	4.2g	0.7g	2.8g

COMFORTING MASH

Page 290

ENERGY	FAT	SAT FAT	PROTEIN	CARBS	SUGARS	SALT	FIBRE
146kcal	2.7g	1.3g	4g	27.9g	2.4g	0.2g	4.9g

GARLICKY GREENS

Page 291

ENERGY	FAT	SAT FAT	PROTEIN	CARBS	SUGARS	SALT	FIBRE
56kcal	3.6g	0.6g	3.1g	2.9g	2.1g	0.2g	1.4g

SLOE GIN POACHED PLUMS

Page 292

ENERGY	FAT	SAT FAT	PROTEIN	CARBS	SUGARS	SALT	FIBRE
392kcal	15.3g	5.1g	5.7g	50.7g	29g	0.4g	2.1g

SMOKED SALMON OAT BLINIS

Page 298

ENERGY	FAT	SAT FAT	PROTEIN	CARBS	SUGARS	SALT	FIBRE
334kcal	10g	2.9g	19.3g	44.5g	7.8g	1.6g	3.9g

EPIC MIXED ROAST

Page 302

ENERGY	FAT	SAT FAT	PROTEIN	CARBS	SUGARS	SALT	FIBRE
335kcal	17.8g	6.6g	34g	9.2g	2.8g	0.6g	1g

VEGGIE CROWN

Page 304

ENERGY	FAT	SAT FAT	PROTEIN	CARBS	SUGARS	SALT	FIBRE
532kcal	24.8g	9.4g	12.8g	67.8g	10.8g	1.3g	5.8g

AMAZING HASSELBACK POTATOES

Page 310

ENERGY	FAT	SAT FAT	PROTEIN	CARBS	SUGARS	SALT	FIBRE
378kcal	15g	3.8g	13.8g	49.2g	2.2g	1.2g	3.4g

FENNEL GRATIN

Page 312

ENERGY	FAT	SAT FAT	PROTEIN	CARBS	SUGARS	SALT	FIBRE
134kcal	10g	5.4g	4.2g	8g	0.8g	0.5g	2.8g

BEAUTIFUL BRUSSELS

Page 314

ENERGY	FAT	SAT FAT	PROTEIN	CARBS	SUGARS	SALT	FIBRE
76kcal	3.6g	0.6g	3.5g	9.9g	3.1g	0.3g	3.9g

DELICIOUS CARROTS

Page 316

ENERGY	FAT	SAT FAT	PROTEIN	CARBS	SUGARS	SALT	FIBRE
62kcal	1.9g	1.1g	1.2g	11.1g	6g	0.4g	2.9g

VEGGIE GRAVY

Page 318

ENERGY	FAT	SAT FAT	PROTEIN	CARBS	SUGARS	SALT	FIBRE
103kcal	2.6g	1.1g	1.8g	16.1g	7.6g	0.4g	1.5g

BANANA PANETTONE PUDDING

Page 320

ENERGY	FAT	SAT FAT	PROTEIN	CARBS	SUGARS	SALT	FIBRE
363kcal	13.8g	8g	7.7g	53.8g	40.8g	0.4g	1.3g

THANK YOU

Writing a book takes a lot of time, and a lot of effort, and I'm extremely lucky to have a wonderful team of people who support me through the entire process, from initial conception, through to shooting, testing, editing, design and production, as well as the whole world of stuff that happens beyond the creative part, getting the book out there and into your hands.

It's a real team effort, and I feel an incredible amount of gratitude to each and every one of the people named on this page. Of course, this is just scratching the surface, and there are many more brilliant people and teams that contribute in some way, shape or form – I hope you all know that you have my love and respect, as ever.

On the food front, thanks to my team of loyal warriors, bringing ideas, inspiration and creativity to the table, and providing endless support. At the helm, one-of-a-kind Ginny Rolfe, and the rest of the brilliant team, Jodene Jordan, Maddie Rix, Elspeth Allison, Rachel Young, Hugo Harrison, Julius Fiedler and Sharon Sharpe. Keeping us all in check, Becky Merrick, Lydia Lockyer and Helen Martin. And our extended food family, on this project Isla Murray, Sophie Mackinnon, Max Kinder, Sarah Tildesley and Francesca Paling. And to two people I'd always invite to my table, Pete Begg and Bobby Sebire. Thank you also to cocktail maestro J Rivera, for helping me simplify and reimagine the drinks chapter. And to green-fingered wonder Graeme Corbett, for the beautiful blooms.

My nutrition and technical food teams do a fantastic job in working with me to be creative and joyful, putting solid nutrition, ethics and standards at the forefront, and on this book, all due respect to Rozzie Batchelar and Lucinda Cobb.

On words, big love to my editor and mind reader Rebecca Verity, to Jade Melling, who's doing a cracking job of creating organization in the chaos, to Beth Stroud and the rest of the team.

Over on design, more big love for my main man James Verity – another beautiful-looking book, brother, and still that sock game is strong. Thanks to you, Barnaby Purdy and the rest of the team. And to our friends at Superfantastic.

Now when it comes to photography, this book has been a bit of a joy for me as I've been lucky enough to work with three of the best in the business, each of whom has brought something different to the table, but who together have created the most visually rich imagery for you to enjoy. I would like to shower you equally with love and respect, David Loftus, Levon Biss, and Paul Stuart. And of course, Richard Clatworthy, who's done a very valiant job assisting you all.

Shout out as ever to talented Lima O'Donnell, Julia Bell and Abbie Tyler for doing their thing – you know how much I appreciate you all.

On to Penguin Random House, who are a great publisher personified. I have an incredible amount of love for all the team. It's like any good marriage – comfortable but we keep each other on our toes when we need to! It's about the give and take and not taking each other for granted. You know I'm ever so grateful. Much respect to Tom Weldon, Louise Moore, Juliette Butler, Katherine Tibbals, Lee Motley, Sarah Fraser, Nick Lowndes, Elizabeth Smith, Amy Davies, Clare Parker, Ella Watkins, Christina Ellicott, Rachel Myers, Deirdre O'Connell, Natasha Lanigan, El Beckford, Louise Blakemore, Chantal Noel, Anjali Nathani, Vanessa Forbes, Kate Reiners, Ines Cortesao, Jane Kirby, Lee-Anne Williams, Jade Unwin, Chris Wyatt, Tracy Orchard, Stuart Anderson, Carrie Anderson, Anna Curvis, Sarah Davison-Aitkins and Catherine Knowles. And much love as always to dear Annie Lee, to Jill Cole, Emma Horton and Caroline Wilding.

Back to JO HQ, I'm fortunate to be surrounded by an amazing bunch of talented people on a daily basis. All my teams are wonderful and contribute so much. Calling out a few people here that directly impact the book, but you know you're all part of this. Thanks to Jeremy Scott, Laura Ball, Michelle Dam and team, Saskia Wirth, Heather Milner, Subi Gnanaseharam and team, Rich Herd and team, Kirsty Dawkins, Louise Holland, Zoe Collins, Sean Moxhay, and of course, Ali Solway.

I'm really excited about the TV show that will accompany this book. We're printing before all the team is confirmed but you know I love you. Big respect to Sam Beddoes, Katie Millard, Niall Downing, their brilliant teams and all the wonderful crew. Love and respect as ever to Channel 4 and Fremantle.

Finally my multi-faceted family who've revealed a whole array of additional talents over the last year. Head teacher and camera woman extraordinaire, my beautiful wife Jools, dear Pops and Daisy, who are headed out into the world, making their own way. And to my little cover stars Petal, Buddy and River, who have brought such a lot of joy into lockdown, and delivered on the cuddles. To my precious Mum and Dad, Anna-Marie and Paul, Mrs Norton and Leon – I can't wait until we can all be together again. And to my mate, Mr Gennaro Contaldo, why is his cooking so good?

INDEX

Recipes marked V are suitable for vegetarians; in some instances you'll need to swap in a vegetarian alternative to cheese such as Parmesan. (Some recipes also include VEGGIE LOVE swap ins, these are marked ✳.)

For a quick reference list of all the vegetarian, vegan, dairy-free and gluten-free recipes in this book, visit:

jamieoliver.com/together/reference

THE JAMIE OLIVER COLLECTION

HUNGRY FOR MORE?

For handy nutrition advice, as well as videos, features, hints, tricks and tips on all sorts of different subjects, loads of brilliant recipes, plus much more, check out

JAMIEOLIVER.COM   #JAMIESTOGETHER

MICHAEL JOSEPH

UK | USA | CANADA | IRELAND | AUSTRALIA | INDIA | NEW ZEALAND | SOUTH AFRICA

Michael Joseph is part of the Penguin Random House group of companies,
whose addresses can be found at global.penguinrandomhouse.com

Penguin
Random House
UK

First published 2021

001

Copyright © Jamie Oliver, 2021

Photography copyright (see below page references) © David Loftus, 2021; © Levon Biss, 2021; © Paul Stuart, 2021

© 2007 P22 Underground Pro Demi. All Rights Reserved, P22 Type Foundry, Inc.

The moral right of the author has been asserted

Photography by David Loftus, Levon Biss & Paul Stuart

David Loftus: pp. 10, 11, 13–17, 21–61, 103, 111–13, 118, 135–53, 166, 209, 226–54, 255, 257–63, 275, 282–7, 290–321
Levon Biss: pp. 82–102, 103, 105–10, 115, 119–33, 156, 157, 159–65, 166, 167, 172, 173, 184–208, 211–21, 324–6, 328–31, 333
Paul Stuart: pp. 5, 10, 11, 18–19, 64–79, 157, 169, 172, 173, 175–83, 223, 255, 266–74, 276–9, 360

Cover photography by Paul Stuart

Design by Jamie Oliver Limited

Colour reproduction by Altaimage Ltd

Printed in Germany by Mohn Media

The authorized representative in the EEA is Penguin Random House Ireland,
Morrison Chambers, 32 Nassau Street, Dublin D02 YH68

A CIP catalogue record for this book is available from the British Library

ISBN: 978–0–241–43117–7

penguin.co.uk

jamieoliver.com

www.greenpenguin.co.uk

Celebrating 22 years of cooking and reading